Dr. John Garang de Mabior Atem: Portrait of an African Freedom Fighter

Edward Abyei Lino

The publisher wishes to acknowledge and thank Dr. Douglas H. Johnson for his invaluable help and support for Africa World Books and its mission of preserving and promoting African cultural and literary traditions and history. Dr. Johnson and fellow historians have been instrumental in ensuring that African people remain connected to their past and their identity. Africa World Books is proud to carry on this mission.

All rights reserved. It is illegal to reproduce, duplicate or transmit any part of this book in either electronic means or printed format. Recording of this publication is strictly prohibited. No part of this publication may be reproduced, stored in a retrieval system, or transmitted, in any form, or by any means, electronic, mechanical, photocopying, recording or otherwise, without the prior permission of the publishers.

Copyright © 2024 Edward Abyei Lino

ISBN: 9781763683969 (Paperback)
9781763683952 (Hardcover)

This book is sold subject to the conditions that it shall not, by way of trade or otherwise, be lent, re-sold, hired out or otherwise circulated without the publisher's prior consent in any form of binding or cover other than in which it is published and without a similar condition including the condition being imposed on the subsequent purchaser.

Cover design, typesetting and layout: Africa World Books
Unit 3, 57 Frobisher St, Osborne Park, WA 6017
P.O. Box 1106 Osborne Park, WA 6916

Dedicated to Atong Garang de Mabior Atem

Garang that fruitful tree
was the one that whoever introduced you unto us
May you step into his footsteps

Contents

1. In Search of a Fitting Epitaph — 9
2. Living my Riddle — 11
3. The Art of Shouldering a Patriotic Agenda — 14
4. From Wangulei's Grasslands of Jonglei — 18
5. A Teacher in Kenya — 20
6. John Garang: Who Was He? — 26
7. The Birth of the Movement — 33
8. Plotting the Revolution in Khartoum — 38
9. Underground Activities in Khartoum — 47
10. The SPLM/SPLA's Birth Pangs — 56
11. Charting a Revolutionary Roadmap — 62
12. From a Modest Beginning to National Stewardship — 69
13. A New Dimension to Politics — 74
14. Meeting His Last Surviving Maternal Aunt — 82
15. Priming for a Tough Mission — 87
16. Garang and Politicians from the South — 96
17. The Pool of Ideas: Which Way, Sudan? — 109
18. Anti-Garang Forces Determined to Destroy Him — 116
19. John Garang: A Portrait of an Astute Thinker — 120
20. Humility and Altruism Defined Garang — 129
21. The Man and his Style — 134
22. Among Neighbours — 143
23. Economic Direction — 149

25. Commander in Chief in Action	164
26. SPLA Incursion into Western Equatoria	169
27. Impediments in the Bush	179
28. Time for Relaxation	182
29. Garang and the World of Ideas	185
30. Inside the Movement	187
31. A Monument to the Cause of Freedom	194
32. Nurturing Foreign Relations	199
33. In Search of a Fitting Epitaph	212
Acronyms and Abbreviations	215

1

In Search of a Fitting Epitaph

His death on July 30, 2005, was but the fall of a political saviour. It was in Khartoum where six million people assembled and intermingled in the city with about twelve million hands held up sky high. Knitting, harnessing, combing and frantically harping that, so harmoniously, candidly, happily with sincerity. In that show, people shed tears of joy, desperately dashing to welcome the humblest son of our beloved land, who loved the soil.

People swarmed in what could be described as some form of 'organised anarchy', raised their palms, waving, shouting, swinging, dancing, ululating and offering praise to heaven: "Now peace has come! Peace has come!"

History has it inscribed that on July 8, 2005, when Dr John Garang de Mabior landed in Khartoum, he was the man of the hour. Surely, multitudes after multitudes poured out in a huge unprecedented human ocean to embrace the man. In that unpolluted atmosphere people were free to meet a free man, the freedom fighter. Those loud antiwar voices rang out on a memorable day, the day of salvation and dawn of peace. It was a day in which Sudan ceased to be the same country we and the rest of the world had known. The great day the downtrodden citizens had finally arrived.

Alas, that wonderful gift from God, if one may assume, was with us briefly before the mission was accomplished. He was snatched from us in the dust of that helicopter crash. To be told that Garang was dead was at first shocking as well as unbelievable. He was bitterly mourned by those who loved him and his vision for his country. Several countries lowered their national banners for three days. Kenya and Uganda mourned for forty days with his portraits displayed on some cities' roundabouts, predominantly in Nairobi and Kampala. That was how the man was recognised. We should not deceive ourselves that he has not died. We know he is dead, but at the same time we persist to believe he is alive, simply because of the belief that the great of this world do not end the way we perish. Heavy clouds may at times obscure sunlight, but ultimately the sun shines.

Today, after a few years since the man left us in this world there are voices, which started to express contemptuousness and take him for the one responsible for all the miseries that befell all the people, without knowing him even. Those were the hopeless voices of the lonely that do not know who they are. The voices of the aimless would not know what to do, where they came from or where they were heading. Death has taken him away prematurely from us. There are mountains of gifts Garang left for us to benefit from. But as we intentionally forgot his gifts, we shall remain day and night, killing one another on the lonely lanes of shame. May God bless those who refuse to know Dr John Garang de Mabior Atem, especially, those who are from his home area.

2

Living my Riddle

Personally, I was shocked and deeply saddened by the loss that had befallen the people of South Sudan. I could not comprehend my exclusion by Cdr Salva Kiir, whom we accompanied with Dr Cirino Hiteng, the manager of the office of the First Vice President, Dr John Garang, to see the Kenyan President Mwai Kibaki at the State House in Nairobi on Sunday evening, July 31, 2005. We went to the State House to receive the condolences of the Republic of Kenya for the tragic loss of John Garang when it was confirmed that he had died. The Kenyan president, Mwai Kibaki arranged for a military plane to fly Cdr Salva Kiir to New Site to view the remains of our departed leader and attend to the meetings pertaining to succession.

We saw Cdr Salva Kiir off the other day from the Kenyan military base to New Site with some members of Garang's family and we followed a day after. At New Site, amid devastating sadness and confusion, I met Alikaya Alhaj Aligo in the presence of Cdr Kuol Manyang Juuk, Cdr Deng Alor Kuol, Cdr Oyay Deng Ajak and others to take part in and conceptualise the design of the mausoleum. And we agreed that Alikaya and I should proceed to Juba to join Cdr Samuel Abu John Kabashi and the committee, which included

Governor Clement Wani and Cdr Thomas Cirillo, to choose the burial spot.

From New Site we were accompanied to Juba by our SPLA guards of honour who escorted Dr John Garang's remains to their destination. The present pentagon-shaped mausoleum, constructed to bear a resemblance to the five-cornered "Guiding Star" in the blue triangle in the national flag was what we chose. Since that time, Cdr Salva Kiir, then Garang's deputy and by then his successor, never talked to me or asked for me, and prohibited me from participating in the investigation process, although I was the director of the external security branch of the movement at the time, exposed to both the senior personnel of Sudanese and Ugandan intelligence services. I was simply excluded for reasons best known to Salva Kiir. I consider my exclusion from those procedures puzzling as well as inexcusable. It is apparent I was the only officer sidelined from the administration of our departed leader, Garang, for baffling reasons.

I was ignored and cast aside, although I expected the SPLM/A to form a team to take part in the investigation. Perhaps, our team might have found a little difference. Since our people would trust our team, for none of them had "a feather stuck in the hair", to use a local South Sudanese metaphor for grandeur. For a different team of investigators to differ, might lead the investigation to unearth the truth. The fact, however, was that the new leader, Salva Kiir opted to turn his back on his national responsibility by not setting a knowledgeable fact-finding team, committed and determined to investigate how we lost our leader, by not recording our loss from our perspective. The result was that it ended the way that we know. With our involvement and participation in probing the cause or causes, the outcome could have been different.

It is normal that weighty crimes stick at the bottom until the pool dries up with time then they will appear. Hence, the longer the time a crime takes in a lee the nearer the suspects might appear.

Some relevant facts might emerge after the case was long hidden in the bosom of darkness. People heard some figures that were about to divulge some leading signals that might lead us to what had happened. Despite that, nothing could alter the doubt about the validity of all the statements made since they fell short of the truth.

Indeed, SPLM has not a single page of story to present to its members, supporters and the public at large, who are interested to know how we lost our leader, the founding leader of the SPLM/A, Dr John Garang de Mabior. Not even a statement was made about how we lost John Garang, or perhaps, a nation was deliberately denied knowing how their leader died. Many people witnessed how different nations mourned Garang, while on the other hand, others surreptitiously celebrated his loss. Under such a situation what one should expect from the millions of compatriots and non-South Sudanese who love and value Garang and what he stood for, is the crafting of a suitable epitaph to preserve his memory for the present and future generations.

Yes, indeed, the SPLM and the Government of South Sudan have every right to conduct a new investigation to re-examine the case. But when will that be done, given the pathetic situation South Sudanese are currently in? There could be some crafty hands involved that might not be interested in revisiting that affair. So, even if some "mighty hands" might have been involved, so what?

3

The Art of Shouldering a Patriotic Agenda

John Garang was one of the outstanding South Sudanese freedom fighters, who gave their lives as youth for the cause of their people. We all lived a life directed by destiny to offer our efforts and freely undertook to do what we did. Garang was a dear comrade in our twenty-two-year- long struggle. His life was eventful, which included the good and the bad a person could be duty-bound to undertake when engaged in a roofless challenge for which people would offer whatever they have including their lives. He had many contacts, which made him the man he became. Garang led the remaking of a new history for the Sudan, when he refused to become a fourth-, a third- or second-class citizen in his country. Hence, he incited the people to either rebuild Sudan for all the Sudanese on an equal basis or never. That was what happened to Sudan in the manner in which he approached the question. His handprints are vividly visible engraved on the contemporary charts of South Sudan and Sudan.

He undertook that process with many colleagues, friends, relatives, acquaintances, as well as enemies. But only a small number of people ventured to record their experiences with Dr John Garang, such as Dr Mansour Khalid, Dr Francis Deng, Dr Wathiq Kameir,

Dr Lual Achuek Deng, General (retired) Lazarus Sumbeiywo, Hilda Johnson and others from overseas with sincerity. Intellectuals saw in him what others did not see. The importance of the role played by John Garang in the contemporary history of Sudan is vital to us, being a man connected to every good a given people would undertake.

Hence, to help people in areas of similar problems, especially along the lines that divide cultures and religions in areas of conflict, the manner and the means to solve conflicts is through peaceful ways, especially in the simmering parts of Africa. The fringes of the sub-Saharan Africa, where Christianity, Islam and different African religious beliefs become sources of rivalry over diminishing resources, are ethnically and doctrinally soaked in bloodshed as was the case in Sudan. So, the experiences of John Garang are treasures people should start collecting.

Therefore, in the coming pages one tends to the national cause, popularly known in Arabic as *dawa* or call, all those knowledgeable about the man to turn their minds, aiming at reflecting their memoirs to think about the experiences Garang left for us to benefit from. Those pages are not chronologically set. These are mere synopses of some aspects of his life. The man is here taken from the point of his interaction with people. And that was how he and I interrelated, as I stood under his shadow during our long struggle together. Garang freely interacted with people, though each person must have different stories, feelings and conclusions from their personal experiences.

Some figures were so close to him but did not gather how the man was marking his steps on the dunes of time. These are normal mergers of thoughts and observations connected to memorable occasions, which constituted part of the life of the man, to kindle our recollections and bring them to life. Some events are presented here to portray how the man sailed through the turbulent storms that characterise political and armed struggle. Struggle was a sacred agenda to Garang and all his compatriots to lay a foundation and pave the way for our young people for them to understand and appreciate that the struggle for justice is costly and that they should be grateful to their forebears in the various roles they played in the quest for freedom with justice.

Garang emerged out of a traditional society denied by geography and history the share of the currents of thoughts that shaped global trends and thought pertaining to the rights of a people to freedom and how to retrieve them after they had been stolen by foreign rulers or suppressed by local autocrats. Garang rose to challenge the way Sudan was patched, as an ailing country. From that reality he tried to convince the world to erect a sound social and legal base for a nation known as South Sudan, through a relentless armed struggle and peaceful ways. Garang tried so hard to rebuild a united country out of its historical realities, on an equitable and just basis. But chauvinists and those with opposing agendas confronted him. Given that blind rejection, and Sudan as a country now broken into two, here we are with a new reality and a new era.

Of the people with whom Garang was acquainted, besides his family, were names one should mention, because of the depth of their relations. His closest associates among the living are Salva Kiir, Pagan Amum, Deng Alor, Oyay Deng, Bior (Aswad) Ajang Duot, James Hoth Mai, Gier Chuang Aluong, Pieng Deng Majok, Yasir Arman Saeed, Malual Majok Chiengkuach, Atem Garang Dau and an array of friends from other parts of the world, among them, Brian D'Silva, Dan Eiffe, Roger Winter, Dan Callery. The list could not be complete without the inclusion of his bodyguards and signal operators. These and other individuals who had known or worked together with John Garang are a rich treasure trove of information about the SPLM/A leader and his thoughts and actions during the twenty-two years we spent together.

President Omar Bashir, with whom Garang became a partner after long enmity, said about his Vice President, Garang, in August 2005 after his death, "I knew him as a fighter. I knew him as a negotiator, and I knew him as a human being." That was Garang. The man deserves a museum similar to the one conceptualised by Alikaya Aligo in 2005, the time the SPLM/A was expected to collect all the relevant portraits, objects and documents where no monuments exist since the Anglo-Egyptian Condominium administration dismantled the ivory-adorned pyramid-like mound of Ngun Deng in Wat between 1927 to 1928 and disposed of it the way they know, which people can still claim. Sincerely, this is a genuine patriotic cause to all the people who knew Garang to meet the challenge and help our people collect what we know about the man. Following the unique history of our being along the Nile, Garang could be a spectacular pyramid, metaphorically speaking.

4

From Wangulei's Grasslands of Jonglei

John Garang de Mabior Atem was born in Aborom (*Abörȫm* in Dinka) village Wangulei, around 1946 according to his own estimate. His mother was Gak Malual Kuol and his father Mabior Atem Aruei of Awulian clan of Awulian *wut* (a group of clans sharing land) of what is part of today's Nyuak Payam, one of the administrative units within Twic East County. In his family, Garang was number four among eight brothers and sisters. The children of Mabior Atem and Gak Malual Kuol (Garang's siblings) in order of their seniority were: Akuol (sister), Aruei, Areng (sister), Atem, Deng, Garang, Akoi, and Malual. None of them is alive.

Wangulei was elevated after 2005 to a *payam* (a local government tier below a county) in the eastern part of Kongor, a new county to the northern part of the former Bor District. Like many villages of South Sudan, the name Wangulei signifies no more than a name to hear in the elephant grass stretching throughout the grazing area dotted with trees, scattered homesteads, and cattle camps, especially during wet seasons.

In dry seasons, except for infants, elderly and the infirm, the community would move with cattle to the swampland—known as *toc*, anglicised as *toich*—to the west. On a carpet of lush pastures around rivulets dotting the vast swampland on the eastern bank of the White Nile, the inhabitants had plenty of milk, and fish would constitute the main diet virtually throughout the year. People become happy when marking the season with a cultural show, amidst plenty.

Wangulei is a flat savanna environment, flooded during rainy seasons. Main crops consist of sorghum, beans, maize, millet and pumpkin, planted around the scattered homesteads in the area that lies east of the great Sudd. Flocks of colourful birds gather in their thousands at the beginning of the rainy season. At the coming of the dry season, multiple species of game, in an amazing rampage, head westward towards the Nile and spread throughout the Sudd pastureland. Unless one had a previous stay or passage through Wangulei, no person would know whether she or he had reached the village. Wangulei was too scattered for a village.

From 2005 onwards, that relatively little-known tranquil village began to put a new mark in the soil, indicating some growth in the field of agriculture, introduced by Mama Rebecca Nyandeng Chol Atem, the steadfast wife of our departed leader, John Garang. Rebecca Nyandeng dedicated part of her time to encouraging women at Wangulei to cultivate sorghum, maize, yam and some wild vegetables and fruits to have a small market. A school and a health centre have come up with a workshop and a modest powerhouse. Wangulei, that once unknown small village to the outside world, is the cradle where John Garang de Mabior Atem was born. Garang's place of his birth has begun to get inserted into the new maps of his native state of Jonglei in the greater Upper Nile region of the independent South Sudan.

5

A Teacher in Kenya

Garang was a man who came fully prepared militarily and intellectually to lead his people. He was ready almost in every respect. He had extensively read all that he wanted to know about political order and change and understood what he read. His shortcomings at times were that he was practically involved in a highly complex situation, which ran beyond what could be regarded as normal human ability. Like the setting of a formidable movement that led to the birth of a nation, South Sudan. His uncle, Athithi Atem Aruei who was working in Tonj in one of the remote corners of Bahr el Ghazal Province then, took Garang there for education. From Tonj Elementary School, the bright boy was admitted to Bussere Intermediate School, where he tasted and nursed his early love of growing crops on plots of land allotted to the students, who grew crops for their own consumption and earned pocket money for themselves. Garang loved the offer that introduced him and fellow students to the idea of farming and agriculture, which became a lifelong vocation.

From Bussere, Garang was admitted to Rumbek Secondary School and left when he was in Third Year in 1962, when the school was closed because of student unrest. Garang was an inquisitive young man, fond of reading. He read whatever he found. Back in Bor home district, young Garang and two of his colleagues, Lueth Garang Kuany and Majok Ayuen Kuur decided to travel to seek education abroad. The three left Southern Sudan in 1962 and first travelled to Kenya from where Garang and his companions decided to sneak into Ethiopia in early 1963. But Garang was arrested and convicted for being in Kenya illegally, when Kenya had just gained independence from Britain. Garang later said that the new minister for Home Affairs, Oginga Odinga, set him and his fellow Sudanese students free, and he went to Ethiopia from where he later went to the USA.

Garang was given no chance to grow and rise to manhood in his home country. But he grew and developed until he became a determined man abroad, where the young could melt untraceable into different cultures and traditions without a shepherd guiding. But his eyes were focused on specific targets and that helped him greatly to achieve his dreams. His first dream was to pursue education, which he did with distinction, starting from the Central Province in Kenya where chance took him to Nyeri where he was taught to support and prepare himself for further education.

Garang found his way to Dar es Salaam in Tanzania where he completed his high school certificate and was admitted to the University of Dar es Salaam. From there he flew to Grinnell in the United States. In 1971 he graduated in agricultural economics, supervised by Professor John Dawson. He strongly believed that his years in Dar es Salaam were the golden times, in which his mind was opened to politics and to progressive theories of liberation. That was when the University of Dar es Salaam emerged as the capital of African liberation in Africa. It was in that pool Garang found himself swimming in the politics of liberation. He interacted with great thinkers like Walter Rodney plus the leaders of the African struggle such as Dr Agostino Neto, Eduardo Mondlane, Sam Nujoma, Amilcar Cabral and South African liberators. In Tanzania Garang met Yoweri Museveni with whom he exchanged revolutionary ideas in the same compass. Garang considered himself a graduate of what could be branded as Tanzanian School of African Socialism. African Socialism became his political ideology.

From Grinnell in the USA in 1970, Garang returned to Tanzania and visited Uganda where he met Alfred Ladu Gore, later to become a friend, whom he accompanied on a visit to Nairobi. In Nairobi he met many Southern Sudanese in a refugee settlement, on whom he left a good impression about his liberation ideas in his young age. Back in Uganda, Chief Andrea Gore, Alfred Ladu's father, arrived from Southern Sudan to visit his son and invited both Garang and Alfred to visit Lobonok in the southern Bari of Central Equatoria State. That was a golden chance after several years of absence from Southern Sudan.

Garang was an intelligent, amiable young graduate, who was admired for his clear Afro-American consciousness, as articulated by the advocates of the civil rights movement sweeping across the USA in the 1960s. The two young men returned to Kampala, where Garang decided to travel to Loboni to meet Akuot Atem. From there, Garang decided to undergo military training. Even as a young man, his modesty was known by what he wore: slippers, flowery African shirts and chain-smoking cigarettes. Garang admired Jaramogi Oginga Odinga's African-styled dresses, also known as Kaunda suit. He was an avid reader of writings about what was known as the African revolution.

Garang met Colonel Joseph Lagu, the leader and commander in chief of the Southern Sudanese armed resistance movement, the Anya Nya, and is reported to have shown his reservations about the choice of secession as the solution to what was known as the Problem of Southern Sudan. That stand was later expressed in his letter to Colonel Joseph Lagu, the Anya Nya leader. For that reason, Lagu kept an eye on John Garang after the Addis Ababa Agreement under whose terms Garang was absorbed into the Sudanese army with the rank of captain.

When peace talks began in Addis Ababa in 1972, John Garang flew to Addis Ababa after his graduation from Grinnell. In the process of negotiations, Garang wrote an elaborate letter to Major General Lagu in which he expressed his opinion against what was arrived at in Addis Ababa, in March 1972. Time proved Garang to be right in 1983, when Nimeiri unilaterally abrogated the Addis Ababa Agreement, justifying his action by saying it was not sacrosanct like the Bible or Quran.

John Garang's relations with Joseph Lagu, the former Anya Nya leader, had been prickly even before the 1972 agreement that ended the conflict between the South and the central government in Khartoum. After his absorption at the rank of captain in the army, Garang was constantly followed by the military intelligence. Aware of that fact, he was always careful in whatever he did or said or the company he kept. That marked his life until he returned to the bush on May 16, 1983.

When Garang departed for the bush and was declared to be the person leading the rebellion, SPLM/A President Nimeiri sent for his deputy director in the research department, Lieutenant Colonel Mahgoub Nasir. Nimeiri wanted to know what had incited him to turn against the government when he had just returned from America and obtained his PhD, which he thought was enough to persuade Garang not to join any rebellion. Lieutenant Colonel Mahgoub Nasir answered the President in a meeting of the high military command and various heads of departments of the Sudanese army.

Lieutenant Colonel Mahgoub Nasir is said to have told him Garang had left because he was frustrated with the way we handled things related to the South. For instance, Garang opposed the imposition of Sharia laws and *kasha*, the forceful removal from Khartoum of jobless citizens from the peripheries, and the random arrests of women for brewing alcoholic drinks to sell for their livelihood and to support the education of their children. Also, Garang did not see any logic in the Sudanese State ordering the inscription of a Quranic verse on the army pennant, when that institution had members who adhered to other faiths, and most Southern Sudanese were Christian. Few people who knew Garang, including his army colleagues from the North, were surprised when they learned he rebelled for the second time.

After he became the SPLM/A leader, whenever he visited areas he had been before in the bush, Garang would ask for some of his colleagues to recollect his memories about the real changes, which might have occurred in the places he had been in the past. He would ask about areas he had been through during his training as a cadet and made friends and acquaintances. When he returned to the Sudan, Garang had a short time to recap, grasp and understand different types of social, political and military issues, squabbles and challenges in the different segments of Sudanese communities, diverse as they were. In short, he studied the composition of the Sudanese people in a manner which no Southern politician had ever done before.

There are those who believe that knowing the language of other people would mean having mastered every aspect of how people do things and begin to demean those with little knowledge, without capturing the history. But Garang studied and knew the history and the composition of the Sudanese people. He took to learning Arabic and had a teacher, Daniel Kodi Angelo, to be able to communicate effectively with his forces in colloquial Arabic and read and intercept messages in the first place. He told his comrades that knowledge of any language, including the language of one's enemy, offers several advantages, including knowing directly what they say, think or do. That fact, Garang said, includes fluency in Arabic, which is the official language of Sudan and its ruling class. Garang was open to learning Arabic and requested some of the comrades who were fluent in standard Arabic to teach him to improve his knowledge of that medium. Within a couple of years, Garang was heard to be narrating news reports—in standard Arabic—he heard over Radio Omdurman.

From his position as the leader of the SPLM/A, Garang had to know people from various ethnicities and understand their problems before he could talk about how to solve them. For example, he learnt about the Rashaida people of eastern Sudan, before he could talk about their problems. He knew the origins of the Ikk, commonly referred to as Teus, of Cushitic like the Uduk and the Nuba. To see the people firsthand, Garang visited them on the top of Mount Lozolia (Zulia) before he could talk about the Ikk on that steep rocky end of South Sudan-Uganda borderlands. But as fate would have it, it was on that same southwestern escarpment of Mount Lozolia, John Garang and company met their fate.

6

John Garang: Who Was He?

In February 1974, I happened to have been detained in Rumbek by the national security agents. I was teaching in Rumbek Senior Secondary School, teaching English and the history of modern Europe from Bismarck to the unification of Germany, World War I and World War II, covering the rise of the Bolsheviks in Russia under Lenin and Stalin, to final year students preparing to sit for the Sudan School Certificate that year. Perhaps, those were the most devastating wars in human history. I was sharing a house with my dear friend, the late Bol Kolok from Pachong, in Rumbek. He was teaching biology to science classes. Bol talked to me about a certain John Garang whom I had never met. My history classes were interesting to students, a group of youths with whom I shared similar revolutionary sentiment at that time. History as a subject—if objectively taught—can be capable of kindling radical intellectual thinking in young persons, to use shattering past events for remodelling the situation in their own time.

In my classes, I used to brief students with the latest news of the day and general knowledge of interest since radio sets were few. I gave such briefings before or after my lessons, to enliven my modules.

The students were so happy and satisfied with my classes. There was nothing more satisfying than students responding positively to the teacher. But stories began to spread from some of my envious colleagues, who alleged that I was teaching students communism and that I was spoiling and misleading the young people. Eventually, I was arrested and dragged into jail without my accusers ever taking the trouble to find out what I was teaching. Concocted by some elements whose candidates lost the 1973 elections and wanted to avenge the failure of their candidate, Samuel Aru Bol, in favour of Malath Joseph Lueth Malath, whom I supported and who won. It became known most of the students voted for Malath Joseph, my favoured candidate whom they supported, to my satisfaction.

We were transported under heavy escort to prison in Wau, with some of my students alleging that we were "dangerous Communists", though none of our capturers knew what communism was about. Ignorant anti-communists gone stupid would make false accusations against communists as people were against moral values of human society. So were we transported under heavy escort to a bigger prison. While I was in jail in Wau, Mathiang Malual Mabur unexpectedly dropped in to visit me to disclose his intention to marry my beloved sister, Anne Nyandeng Wuor Abyei, alias Nyanthon. I had closely known Mathiang since my days in Khartoum and happened to put up with them in 1967 at the residence of Uncle Manoah Majok, who was my father's friend.

I accepted Mathiang Malual's proposal on condition that Nyanthon should convey her consent to me, since Joseph Dut, our elder brother, was in Khartoum. After two days I was admitted to hospital with severe malaria. After my third day in the hospital, my prospective brother-in-law told me that his days were numbered, and the wedding should be approaching. But Nyanthon told him she would not wed since her brother was still under arrest and in hospital. We discussed that matter and searched for the best way to jump over that little hurdle. I came to suggest to him that it would be best for the wedding party to visit me in the hospital direct from church to enable me to congratulate them after the matrimony. They both agreed.

Mathiang Malual willingly accepted that suggestion and it was done in that way. But as I was talking to my sister, accompanying relatives, friends and ladies who were ululating and wailing beside the bride, I told them: "I am here under arrest; I am not a thief or a criminal. I am here because of this land. Now you may go. Indeed, I am honoured, greatly delighted and happy with you all. Congratulations!"

Everybody around looked down for a moment listening, except my brother-in-law, Lieutenant Mathiang Malual and his best man, Captain John Garang de Mabior, who gazed at me while spreading a broad smile on his youthful face.

That smile of Captain John Garang captured my feelings and I felt that he was telling me, "Well done, we shall meet again." That entourage departed amidst flowing ululations. I was so elated and extremely pleased to receive them, driving a long wedding party from the church to pass by me in the hospital. That was the first time for me to witness a wedding celebration accompanied with ululations taking place within the precinct of a hospital of all places. And it was, indeed, an unforgettable honour from a brother-in-law to a brother under detention and hospitalised!

But that was not our first encounter. A few days before the wedding, Captain John Garang happened to visit me in hospital in the company of Major Jibril Makoi Abdallah, who was a dear friend to me. Jibril introduced Garang to me as one of his close friends. They took time laughing about their Anya Nya days in the bush. At that point I asked myself, "Why is this man friendly to all my closest friends?" I felt an inexplicable kind of magnetism that was pulling me towards his personality, eloquence and depth of thoughts. When

George Maker, one of my most trusted friends, visited me a day later, I confided in him at having been introduced by Major Jibril Makoi to Captain John Garang and on how warm their visit was. George went on to disclose to me more information about Garang. General Joseph Lagu and Major Abul Gasim Mohammed Ibrahim had held a meeting in Bussere, where they seemed to have decided to transfer Captain John Garang from there to Bor.

My friend George Maker told me that Captain John Garang was the only Anya Nya officer with a university degree from Iowa University in the USA. He organised the forces, guided and trained them in how to supplement their income by growing vegetables and raising poultry for sale as well as for consumption by their families. Captain John Garang seemed to have decided to stand and assist his colleagues at the most difficult time of transforming their lives, on how to depart living the way they lived in the bush and adopt a new way of life guided by specified income during peace. The oscillation between elastic requirements and specific income was a challenge not only to people coming from the bush, but also to those who were in towns, where money counts most.

Maker Benjamin told me how Garang had organised and encouraged his forces to do very useful things to supplement their meagre incomes and develop their knowledge. Captain Garang began to open classes to teach some of them, of whom Captain Salva Kiir was one. He succeeded to liberate his colleagues and soldiers from one of our social habits. The habit of accommodating relatives and friends for free while contributing nothing useful to the hosts, was one of the behaviours that he said should be discouraged. In support of that he often quoted the Tanzanian leader Julius Nyerere's famous saying, "If you have a guest in your house, you may accommodate and feed him for three days and after that give him a hoe to join you in the farm. Why would you feed somebody or house a person for free?" Captain John Garang would sometimes tease his colleagues.

Maker Benjamin and I discussed the issue of dependency and resolved to discuss it further with Garang, as one of the habits people should avoid changing their lives, in big towns like Wau. We failed to meet Garang. Our intention was to do something practical. But he was transferred from Bussere to Bor, and we were instructed to return to the university after the unrest, which clamped it down. But we had all agreed with Captain Garang that unjustified dependency was a habit that should not be encouraged at all. That type of behaviour directly encourages idleness and makes such "dependents" a burden on their hosts, the relatives they sponge on.

George Maker and I were fully aware that the envy and racial arrogance of the Northern Sudanese towards Captain John Garang in Bussere could have been the reason why senior military figures such as Major Abul Gasim Mohammed Ibrahim, a member of Revolutionary Council under Major General Jaafar Mohammed Nimeiri, flew from Khartoum to Wau to investigate such rumours without the knowledge of General Joseph Lagu, who was bitter about what Captain John Garang was doing in the army at Bussere. We suspected that one of his two-faced colleagues might have been spying on him for Khartoum. We agreed that was nothing but envy. We went back to history, especially to that case of Captain Alfred Dreyfus, a French artillery officer of Jewish ancestry, who was convicted of treason, which became a maxim in modern armies. Applied to the case of John Garang, there are similarities: a junior officer at the rank of a captain–in this case, John Garang- winning a case against a senior officer such as General Joseph Lagu given the time and space in which they were confronting one another.

Major John Garang stuck to that way of helping himself with cultivation. Before he was transferred to Bor, he decided to buy and send home a tractor instead of buying a car as done by almost all the Sudanese who were abroad for courses or scholarships. There in Bor he surprised the people with his tractor. He drove it himself and had a modest vegetable garden. He had a good harvest and sold his products for a modest price. Garang only bought a new car the time he was transferred to Khartoum, which he also left parked with the late Daniel Deng Yong, popularly known as Deng-Majaang to deliver to Dr Gasim Badri, the principal of Al Afhad College for Girls, when he decided to join the bush. Despite being the leader of a political and military movement, a lofty position that placed him on a par with a head of state, Garang brought a tractor to Boma area and started to farm for his forces. It was a sizeable farm comprising sorghum, maize, cassava, green-gram, sweet potatoes and other varieties of vegetables. Garang was a budding academic, a professional soldier and a remarkable farmer rolled into one.

Our concern—George Maker and I—was for Captain Garang to stick to the army and avoid confronting his seniors, who tend to be confrontational over trifles. Especially with his being among the few university graduates in the army with all the sensitivities about his intellectual superiority as a Southern Sudanese, which placed him ahead of many of his other colleagues, and graduates of military college. As a habit, senior officers in the armies tend to be absolute with what they believe. We advised him to make a real difference to compensate for Southerners who were not accepted in another army branch and the judiciary, for instance. We liked him to lead in the army, which was the tool the ruling class had been using for suppressing the marginalised peoples of Sudan, especially Southerners, since that mutiny under the umbrella of the White League, led by First Lieutenant Ali Abdel Latif was nipped in the bud in 1924.

In February 1974, I was discharged from Wau hospital. After we staged a five-day hunger strike in prison we were finally released from detention. Captain Garang invited George Maker and me to the officers' club in Wau, in the former residence of Uncle Stanislaus Paysama Abdallah. After that dinner we fixed other appointments to discuss some aspects related to Sudanese history. Garang used to take notes about issues that interested him. Since I knew Garang, I sensed him to be fond of taking notes. Whenever he came across something he believed to be of importance, wherever he was, Garang took notes and never forgot them. With him, one became closer like being prepared by destiny to join hands in pursuance of a grand cause.

7

The Birth of the Movement

From the time Garang was in Wau as a captain to the time he became a colonel, we did not meet, until 1982. From Wau, Captain Garang was transferred to Command Battalion 105 in Bor. From Bor he was sent to undertake a course in Fort Benning in the USA and returned to Sudan in 1975. Major Garang was transferred to become an instructor in the Sudan's Military College. In 1978, Lieutenant Colonel Garang was permitted to register for his PhD at Iowa State University, supervised by Professor John Francis Timmons. He completed it successfully and returned to Khartoum in 1981 where he was attached to the operations department in the Army general headquarters. Later, he was transferred to head the Sudanese Military Research Unit. In Khartoum in 1981, Dr John Garang taught at the Faculty of Agriculture besides his previous assignment in the army, until he departed for the bush on May 16, 1983.

We kept following one another through verbal messages. Garang came to Juba, around January or February 1982. Our group invited him for dinner in the Unity Garden. We were Benjamin Bol Akok, chairman of NAM; Sirr Anai Kelueljang, for communication; Edward Lino Abyei, for organisation; Amon Wantok to oversee Bahr el

Ghazal; George Maker Benjamin, for Lakes Province; and Marko Chol Machiech, for finance. That part of the leadership who attended the dinner were pleased to be present on that historic occasion, as the steering committee of the underground body, NAM. We were excited to meet our Chief of Staff of the National Action Movement Liberation Army (NAMLA), Dr John Garang.

But when many people gathered in Gore, Ethiopia, most of the founding members and the leadership of NAM were not around. Most of the leaders were either delayed on the way, or opted to form their own organisations or left and became untraceable. It was not a distance one could travel to with ease. John Garang was confronted with that reality and agreed with the rest of the conferees and chose a new name for the movement and named it: the Sudan People's Liberation Movement or SPLM, for short. That name would engulf all the other movements in Southern Sudan on an equal basis. That was the reason NAM was clearly indicated in the manifesto, as one of the progressive movements with clearly articulated vision. The SPLM/SPLA was set as a progressive liberation movement, open to all the people including Northern Sudanese as provided in the manifesto.

That same evening Garang was briefed, as since he left for America things had begun to deteriorate in Sudan in general and in the South in particular. That was the reason we decided to assign him the responsibility of Chief of Staff of NAMLA (National Action Movement Liberation Army). And Garang accepted his new assignment and added the importance of recruiting some colleagues and acquaintances from the former Anya Nya who were reliable and ready to join NAMLA, such as Colonel Yohannes Yor, and Colonel Edward Peter, Colonel George Hilal, Lieutenant Colonel Daniel Awet and Captain Salva Kiir among others. The rest of the former Anya Nya officers were distracted by other personal issues and were untraceable.

We all knew that Colonel John Garang, because of secrecy, would pursue the serious mission of contacting some of his former Anya

Nya colleagues, which he took to be his duty. The people whose names he gave us, by way of example, were later invited by him to respond to the national call. The first to join him was Captain Salva Kiir followed by Daniel Awet Akot. The rest delayed until they died. We began to feel that time had started to approach the zero hour for the movement to kick off.

During that dinner, the group briefed Garang that some comrades had met Othwonh Dak, the commissioner of Upper Nile, in Malakal and had insisted on going to the bush since we were delaying. And they left under Lokurnyang, Ngachigak Nyachiluk and Pagan Amum towards Boma Hills in the Pibor area. Comrades within their internal cell briefed Garang of the on comrades who became restless and contacted William Abdalla Chuol in Pan-gak and Atem Garang Kuek, who was the district commissioner at Akobo. Approaching midnight, our sitting ended and each of us departed discretely. At that stage we concluded that historic working dinner.

A few days later, Garang travelled to Khartoum, but returned after a couple of months and proceeded to Bor. He briefly stayed with Major Kerubino Kuanyin Bol, who was coming from his command post at Pochalla, passing through Bor on his way to Juba. The two officers travelled separately to Juba according to their plan. Where they met before they returned to Bor, preceded by John Garang, who was accompanied by his family during the last week of April 1983. In those days, there was a nagging feeling among some of us, that an event of historic proportion was about to explode. However, the time for that to happen was the question: when?

During the first week of May 1983 in Juba, the two army officers, Garang and Major Kerubino Kuanyin Bol, met and agreed on a plan. Kerubino Kuanyin was to see Major General Siddiq al Banna, the officer commanding the Sudan Armed Forces in the Southern Region, based in Juba, to whom he was to present some elephant tusks and leopard skins he brought to him specially from Pochalla to grease the general's hands, one would say. That was the ploy they used to lure the general to supply them with the required military logistics for the government garrisons in Bor, Pibor and Pochalla. There were credible fears of an imminent attack by Anya Nya Two on Pochalla, expected from around Akobo during that coming wet season. General Siddiq al Banna took it for granted from Major Kerubino Kuanyin, reinforced by the fact that he believed that since the officer was a Dinka from Bahr el Ghazal and not a Nuer or even a Dinka from Bor, given his physical appearance—Kerubino Kuanyin in appearance was a little coffee brown, lighter for a typical Southern Sudan and could be mistaken for a Northern Sudanese—some observers often mistook him for an Arab in racial terms.

General Siddiq al Banna was a narrow-minded, self-indulgent person, who placed acquisition of material benefits above national interests. Banna gratefully welcomed the elephant tusks and supplied Major Kerubino Kuanyin with what he had asked for. Siddiq al Banna bartered the tusks and the hides with ammunition and that was what Southern Sudan meant for him, as far as he was concerned. So, Colonel Garang and Major Kerubino Kuanyin deftly exploited that basic weakness on the part of the general. In that way, Siddiq al Banna, whose apparent innocence and selfishness being turned to an advantage, contributed to the rise of the movement by refusing to talk to his soldiers about reasons accounting for the delay of soldiers' salaries.

In Juba, Colonel John Garang and Major Kerubino Kuanyin decided to pick up the issue of salaries that had been deliberately delayed, to start heating the situation across all ranks. He later told me, "Once pockets were dry that would negatively affect people's minds." But Major General Siddiq al Banna considered that protest to be a form of rebellion and so decided to confront it by force. Right from Juba, to Bor, Pibor, Ayod and Pochalla, the situation began to heat up beyond contention to the time it erupted. Starting from Bor,

Ayod, Pibor and Pochalla, followed by a long chain of defections from Malakal, Kapoeta, Bentiu, Rumbek to Aweil, it largely affected all the organised forces in a solidarity that resulted in the creation of the SPLM/A.

Those defections happened where the former Anya Nya contingents had been told they were going to be transferred to different parts of Northern Sudan, leaving their families without bread winners. That was the time maximum secrecy was required. And both Colonel John Garang and Major Kerubino Kuanyin, kept the top secret to themselves. It was classified as the greatest secret ever, which the people kept ruminating for a long time in their mind—being the emergence of the movement—that would shake Sudan as never before the outbreak of the revolution. That was how the war of liberation started and spread throughout Southern Sudan, Blue Nile and the Nuba Mountains, since May 16, 1983.

8

Plotting the Revolution in Khartoum

While we were in Khartoum, we closely followed the developments when that confrontation began in Battalion 105 in Bor, and the revolution was born. We were organised into a committee, which met weekly in the Faculty of Engineering, University of Khartoum, in the office of Lam Akol. We were Deng Yong, Charles Manyang Awuol, a diplomat, Colonel Gordon Muortat, Major Arok Thon Arok, Major Nikanora Magar Achiek, Peter Nyot Kok, Lam Akol and Edward Abyei (the author). We had affiliates out of Khartoum Sirr Anai, Marco Chol Machiech, Amon Wantok and George Maker Benjamin, who were the founding members of NAM. Our task was to follow, strategise and organise our people to confront whatever might take place with regard to Southern Sudan and prepare ourselves for eventualities and get prepared to lead the people.

We were a selection from a clandestine organisation to confront the May regime when it imposed Sharia laws on the country. We deeply felt that it was our Southern national duty to undertake that responsibility since many Southern politicians, if not all, were grafted and overused by the ailing May regime and were stained by the fading colours of the Sudanese Socialist Union, SSU, which was a strange intermingling of ideological left and right. We were the people who authored that widely distributed public protest, which we delivered to the American Vice President, George Bush, when he visited Sudan to the surprise of President Nimeiri and all his security organs. Later, we all decided to merge into the SPLM/SPLA. In the process we became founding members of the movement that soon turned out to be the biggest challenge to the ruling authorities in Khartoum.

Major Arok Thon Arok was flown from Malakal to Khartoum under arrest, before May 16, 1983. He was with us in our committee before he was transferred to Juba to represent the Army in the People's Regional Assembly for fear to keep him active in the army. Major Arok Thon Arok was highly suspected of being a Trojan horse in respect of the boiling situation in the South, but there was no evidence to substantiate such suspicion when the political status in Sudan deteriorated before the division of Southern Sudan, which he vehemently opposed. They flew him from Malakal and kept him under arrest in Sheijara armoured garrison officers' mess near Lieutenant Colonel Mathiang Malual, Major Nikanora Magar Achiek, Major Chol Ayuak Guiny and First Lieutenant Musa Abdalla Mabok, who were affiliated to us organisationally and considered country-wide to be the most daring officers in the government amoured division.

On the evening of May 16, I went to meet my friend, Major Arok Thon Arok. We embraced for a period longer than was necessary. That was to nullify possible suspicion from his guard, because Arok was whispering to me about what had happened in Bor that day. He informed me that Garang was safe and had withdrawn to the village, heading towards Ethiopian borders with his family. Major Kerubino Kuanyin Bol took part in the fighting but was wounded.

Immediately from there, I had to leave al Sheijara garrison at about six-thirty in the morning with Lieutenant Colonel Mathiang Malual, who also knew what was going on in Bor. Since I had no car,

I asked him to take me to where I had to rush for an appointment. Being my brother-in-law and a friend too, Mathiang Malual took me in his car and willingly accepted to give me that historic lift, when he took me to meet my friend, Ismail Hassan, the consul general at the Ethiopian embassy. I had a previous meeting with Ismail. We knew each other intimately.

I informed Mathiang about my appointment with Ismail. Since Mathiang did not know the address, I directed him. Mathiang understood my urgent mission and stressed its importance. We went straight into his car and drove to Ismail's residence. We parked inside the compound to maintain the necessary secrecy. We briefed Ismail on the military developments in Bor.

I told him, "Colonel Dr John Garang, the man I talked to you about, is now on his way walking all the way with his family to Ethiopia."

He was taken aback, greatly surprised. I promised to keep him always informed about how things were exploding in the South. And things began to develop rapidly. A day later we were informed that people had escorted Major Kerubino Kuanyin to Ethiopia having been wounded in his arm. Ismail Hassan took what transpired in Bor, which involved the head of the military research unit of the Sudanese army to be a very serious matter and a precedence.

On May 23, 1983, Ismail Hassan passed by me in Bahr el Ghazal Coordination Office, Amarat 31st Street at about 12:30 pm and asked for me. As Ismail Hassan was pretending to be asking me for something in the nearby Saudi embassy, he passed me a quick message to meet that evening. Bahr el Ghazal office was infested with intelligence following what had happened in Bor. He told me to meet him that evening with Mathiang Malual at 07:30. Major Arok Thon was still under detention. I informed Mathiang about the appointment and kept Dr Lam Akol in the picture, being one of our comrades, who hosted all the meetings of our resistance committee in his office in the Faculty of Engineering, where we were organising our people with some colleagues in anticipation of the changes in the Sudan before the SPLM/A was conceptualised and born. With Dr Lam Akol, we assisted one another with sincerity respecting our missions to the dot.

We met Consul Ismail Hassan on time and went straight to his residence. Ismail told us he was leaving that same evening for Addis Ababa, and he wanted to take with him a written message from us to his people in Addis Ababa, to explain what was going on in Bor and a word introducing and recommending Dr John Garang, who was at that time in charge of the research unit of the Sudan Army. Ismail stressed that, "His people wanted what he had asked for." And stressed the importance of what he asked for, when we were anticipating the same thing. Ismail Hassan brought me a pen and paper. I sat down to write what he had asked for. Adding that, "Dr John Garang was the very person we spoke about some time ago." I concluded the note with a request, *Thankfully please, let Dr John Garang de Mabior meet your people at the top even if it would be for only five minutes, once he reaches your end safely, and to know from him personally about what is happening in Southern Sudan and Sudan in general.*

I strongly felt that President Mengistu Haile Mariam, a revolutionary leader from an originally oppressed nationality during the reign of an oppressive monarchy, must have a buildup of emotions against oppression. That might persuade him to listen to our call, understand and extend a helping hand to people who stood to liberate themselves like Namibians, Mozambicans, Angolans, Somalis and why not Southern Sudanese? In those days the diplomatic ties between Ethiopia of Mengistu Haile Mariam and the Sudan of Nimeiri were where enmity was inflating and at the verge of explosion. Indeed, it was so hot a time between the two neighbouring countries.

It took Consul Ismail Hassan some days and he returned on May 27, 1983. And Major Arok Thon Arok who was released from detention on May26, a day before Ismail returned and whom I briefed about what went on with the Ethiopians, came with us to be introduced to our great friend Ismail Hassan. We met on time and jumped into Ismail's car and straight to his residence. We arrived at his home and found the main gate open.

Ismail Hassan appeared to be extremely happy, and a soothing wind of satisfaction wafted on me as I was pondering, *Ethiopia must have responded very positively in a relatively short time for those types of contacts like we long for.*

Naturally, my morale soared skyward. It was one of the occasions words failed to express the exact joy I was feeling about the way things had turned out in our favour. I felt as if it was a dream that had come true. Tears of joy were flowing, and I was helpless to control them. Our hopes were becoming a concrete reality: the struggle for the liberation of our people from bondage was becoming a tangible reality. At the time I heard a soothing voice, as if it was coming from above, drowning our conversation with this statement, *Your resolve will immensely help in the liberation of your people in the foreseeable future. Go on. Go on.*

I began to imagine hearing such a reassuring voice and momentarily found myself in a serenity, the moment we entered Ismail's living room.

At the time of our entry, Ismail Hassan rushed, grabbed and embraced me, Lieutenant Colonel Mathiang Malual and Major Arok Thon Arok and firmly held our hands together and shouted, "Mabrouk, Mabrouk. Please, sit down. Sit down. Mabrouk." [*Mabrouk* is the Arabic word for congratulations.] "Everything you have requested has been accepted. Very soon you will receive a confidential message detailing the kinds of assistance our leaders are preferred to offer to meet your requests. They are sending you their fraternal greetings and congratulate you on behalf of your people. Once more, Mabrouk!" an excited Ismail told us. He added that he would brief his bosses in Addis Ababa about our possible physical and active presence there.

In our letter we had requested some assistance to be rendered to Garang on arrival in Ethiopia. I stood and thanked him warmly, by embracing him and so did the rest. We had introduced Major Arok Thon Arok to him. Ismail was so excited to know, Lieutenant Colonel Mathiang Malual and Major Arok Thon Arok were well situated in the Sudanese Army, with easy access to senior people at top state positions, as well as his ties to the intelligence service, introduced him to diplomatic circles of friendly countries. And we found ourselves modestly celebrating, that graceful evening.

Add to that, the respectable social positions of Dr Lam Akol and Dr Peter Nyot in society as reliable researchers. With Ismail Hassan, our relations became more intimate. He introduced us to his bold assistant, Getachew Yusuf and his fair daughter. We were informed that the Ethiopians from their side deployed an intelligence group, whom we later came to know be with the Ethiopian security officials, Abere, Zarihun and Thokwath, as part of their preparation for the reception of Garang along the border, once he appeared. From that date Abere became a real comrade to the movement and to most founding members. And so were Thokwath, the Party Secretary of Gambela and Colonel Zarihun. Besides food, medicine, clothing and shelter, our Ethiopian friends, through Dr John Garang, the clarity of our case and our ability to fight for our rights always endeared us to the Ethiopians. Indeed, Ethiopia offered to our people whatever they wanted from "needles to tanks and human lives," as they put it.

Ethiopia dispatched a helicopter for that mission, and we were informed after the third week of June that *Colonel Dr John Garang and family have safely arrived, had gone through Itang and had a long audience with Colonel Mengistu Haile Mariam, the Ethiopian leader, having crossed the border.* During the last week of June 1983, we were also informed that Garang with some comrades had been taken to Addis Ababa and then to Nazareth, a hundred miles southeast of the capital of Addis Ababa, where they drafted the basic documents in preparation for the formation of the SPLA/SPLM (that order was later reversed to SPLM/SPLA) in 1983. After the Sudan People's Liberation Army/Sudan People's Liberation Movement SPLA/SPLM was formed in Gore, things began to change once people regrouped and organised the basic documents, mainly the movement's manifesto and the Disciplinary Laws of the SPLA.

The movement was born to grow under the name of the Sudan People's Liberation Movement with its military wing, the Sudan People's Liberation Army. The direction and mission of the movement were conceptualised on progressive lines, dedicated to the liberation of the people of Sudan. Garang's resolve was based on his Anya Nya experience and the revolutionary world, to divide in line with the notorious and age-long Northern Sudanese divide and conquer mentality from the start and confuse them more about the direction of the people in Southern Sudan and other marginalised people of the Sudan were heading with regard to the sensitive issue of separation.

The move against secession constituted the rallying point around which all the Arabo-Islamic Northern Sudanese ideological orientation, effectively used to harvest tremendous financial and military support from Muslim Arab and Muslim nations around the world. That time most people who arrived to Bilpam, Itang and Gambela were out for separation and Garang grasped that overwhelming trend so clearly. Garang also understood whatever was going on internationally, starting from Ethiopia, which at the time was fighting against a secessionist in Eritrea. Under those circumstances, our people came to understand and appreciate the willingness of the government in Addis Ababa to assist us in our struggle against the Northern oppression.

So Garang decided to make full use of his presence in Ethiopia, building a force, which would break the back of reactionaries in Khartoum, in the shortest possible time. That desire in Ethiopia, when he embarked on military action, at first appeared to surpass his political dream when he stated, *What we lack is a formidable force to confront the military might Khartoum had been using for long to oppress our people since 1955. We had our political parties and civic organisations. Therefore, we must change our tactic to be able to defeat them.*

Garang knew the importance of building a force free from parochial factors such as ethnic, regional or religious chauvinism that divide people. Garang sought to build the movement on healthy ideas that could help him unite the people throughout the country and build a formidable front to spearhead the revolutionary political and armed struggle. But in that drive, he rarely talked about revolution, but instead he most of the time emphasised the role of liberation to stress the difference between the two words in terms of its relevance to our situation, given the stage of social and political development of our people, which had always been a controversial topic among the intellectuals and urban elites among Southern Sudanese.

In Northern Sudan and in Khartoum specifically, besides our clandestine activities, we briefed students about the performances of the movement and participated in public activities through the Sudan African Congress, (SAC) and others through the National Party under the leadership of Rev. Philip Abbas Gaboush, during the democratic era after Nimeiri was toppled. Rev Gaboush used to agitate the public openly whenever he addressed public rallies and people would stir up whenever they heard the names of Dr John Garang, Cdr Yousif Kuwa, Dr Mansour Khalid and all the fighting comrades, sending them best wishes and greetings from all the slums of Khartoum and the marginalised towns countrywide. That trend rapidly increased the popularity of the movement in the Sudan. At that time, one could see all the marginalised peoples moving to unite.

The Proposed Visit of the Second in Command of SPLM/A

SPLM/A, who ignited the movement in Bor, Major Kerubino Kuanyin, with a battalion to take part alongside other Sudanese political forces of the *intifada* [uprising in Arabic] during a conference in Wad Medani 1985, exploded like a bombshell at the heart of the metropolitan Khartoum. It shook the Transitional Military Council to the marrow, being the people engaged in the war against that very SPLM/A in the South. And to be expected to receive or condone the visit of the second man in the movement to Wad Medani, the second city in the Sudan, close to Khartoum, in fact, would have been quite a contradiction. That move was an intelligent one and so daring, by the leadership of the movement. It was planned to fix the military and the militarists to face the masses and bring war nearer to Khartoum to resolve once and for all, the "Sudanese Problem", not the usual "Southern Problem". Politically speaking, the SPLM/A programme presented a formidable challenge, like never before, to the perception the Northern Sudanese intelligentsia held about the challenges facing the system of rule since independence from Britain in 1956.

9

Underground Activities in Khartoum

In the second year after the movement was formed and military operations started, in which several historic successes were recorded in the battlefield that trembled the Sudanese geo-politics so hard, the country began to change drastically. All the oppressed countrywide began to wake up and raise their voices and tended to be confrontational. They all felt liberated from all sorts of fear in the first place. Every heroic step taken by the movement would irritate the people as if injected with a new spirit of resistance in Khartoum. One example to note was Sergeant Samuel Bol Ajok of the logistics corps in Khartoum North and some of his colleagues in the rest of the garrisons.

Sergeant Samuel Bol Kur and his colleagues planned a coup in Khartoum in which they tried to involve the movement in September 1984. They contacted Rev Philip Abbas Gaboush about the coup and he accepted to patronise the move. Believing the movement had blessed the coup, Rev Gaboush sent me a note written in a small packet of Benson and Hedges cigarettes. At the time I was in the office of Peter Nyot, when we were meeting Colonel Yohannes Yor, coming from Renk with reports about their activities. Many people passed through, going to join the movement. We were meeting Peter Nyot, Yohannes Yor and myself, the time the message from Rev Philip Gaboush was delivered to me by a young lady, who was secretary to Rev Abbas Gaboush. I took the packet, opened and read it. I was astonished. Gaboush was asking me to prepare documents pertaining to the coup being planned. These included:

first, a statement of the coup; second, suggesting a proposal on how the cabinet should be formed, and third, a declaration of a curfew after the success of the takeover. I quietly thanked that young lady and she left.

Surprised as I was, I divulged to the members of the inner circle the top-secret, which that small box contained. It all looked as if the fate of our million-square-mile country, had been squeezed into a small packet of cigarettes! Three of us agreed to stop that premature coup and decided to closely follow their preparedness, in terms of command and political readiness. Three of us decided to ask Colonel Gordon Muortat to come, being the person in charge of our military affairs committee and Major Nikanora Magar Achiek, his deputy. We met that same evening and decided to let Magar ascertain their preparedness and personalities involved to know what was going on. We felt time was running fast though it was, as we observed things around us, moving quite harmoniously. It was a tough move to stop that coup. That was a rare heart-breaking experience, too sudden as it was.

Magar went and met them. He found about six non-commissioned officers (NCOs) and a lieutenant called Yunis Abu Sadur, a young flamboyant officer from the Nuba Mountains, in Rimeila south of Khartoum and came to know some trustworthy officers, among them: Lieutenant Colonel Ramadhan Abugor and Ismail Khamis Jallab and others who did not attend that meeting. The meeting was to review the overall situation, and spell out specific assignments and responsibilities among members. Lieutenant Abu Sadur was in the chair.

Magar returned the next day and was astonished to the extent that he described the idea of the coup as "a big joke", in terms of command and preparedness. He also said that Lieutenant Yunis Abu Sadur and the NCOs were the only individuals who had decided to take power and had deceived Rev. Philip Abbas Gaboush about their readiness. The only thing they were lacking was political leadership to execute their scheme, which he had accepted pending the approval by Garang, who would then take charge. They did that after fixing a date for the coup, without informing Major Nikanora Magar or any one of us. That adventurous group thought and acted recklessly.

From there, I was given the mission to stop the coup by informing Rev. Philip Abbas Gaboush not to go ahead with the plan. I went and delivered him our message to stop the coup and told him that preparations were not complete, to lessen his disappointment and left his residence. Minutes after I had left, Rev. Philip Gaboush was arrested with several others. But he was whisked to a different place while the rest were taken to Kober Prison. The next day Lam Akol and I were arrested, too, and taken to Kober, where we were met by surprise. But the government did not know they had arrested the most senior representative of the movement and his assistant, in charge of contacts; the two biggest fish whom they were surely fishing for in the ocean.

The irony in the situation was the fact that we were both arrested for something we knew, but to which we were not a party and did our best to stop. We both knew about the coup and its masterminds though we did the best we could to stop it. Not only because it was premature, but also because we were both against coups as a matter of principle and according to directives we had received earlier from the headquarters, *not to associate with or take part in any coup or associate with anyone planning a coup.* We had to do our best to disassociate the movement from such adventures aimed at changing the system of rule. During investigation, Lam and I were intensively questioned, each alone, by the security about things to which we were not a party, though we knew what was supposed to happen and what did not and by whom.

Many people were arrested like Mursi Musa, an advocate, those who cooked up the coup in addition to Southern officers like Colonel George Hilal, Lieutenant Colonel Mathiang Malual and Ismail Khamis Jallab. A list of wanted officers was declared over Radio Omdurman and television, which included Lieutenant Colonel Chol Ayuak, Major Nikanora Magar, Lieutenant Laat Benjamin Bil and Abdel Aziz Adam el Hilu and others whom they failed to arrest, except for Lam Akol who was released after some days. The rest of us, numbering 207 in number, spent about four months in jail after which we were taken to court martial at Karari, north of Omdurman, chaired by a notorious Sharia judge, el Makashfi Taha al Kabashi, during the first week of January 1985.

While in court I was asked about my name and address and where I used to stay, to which I responded, "I do not know," to which my colleagues in court responded with laughter. As I sat, a military police guard who appeared to be from western Sudan came closer. Resolute as he was standing, that soldier asked me whether I wanted to go to the restroom. At that moment I was moved and found myself responding to him in the affirmative to his question and he pointed at me to move. We approached a nearby restroom when he whispered to me some few solid words, "Let Kabashi try to pass a judgement and they will see us today. Please furtively alert the rest to be steady." That sweet whisper fell into my ears like a trumpet at midday and I felt warm, as it was delivered unto me.

I received that message and delivered it to the rest of my colleagues in the court very carefully. From among the 207 people accused, nine were to be sentenced to death. I was among the nine. of which I was to be the fourth. The court began by questioning Rev. Philip Gaboush, the first accused, for a few minutes, when a letter was delivered to the court's president by a military scout. Makashfi opened the letter in a hurry and grasped its content. He called the other two members of the panel and they conferred for about five minutes, then ordered the court to resume. He knocked the table hard three times and went on to address the court in a clear disappointed tone, "Listen. His Excellency the President of the Republic has decreed his pardon. He has pardoned all of you. So, you are freed. You may now go. The court is over." With that announcement, we were set free. From there we were all then taken to the security unit where we were cleared and released.

All contacts and activities had to run underground. But I kept contact with Lieutenant Colonel Ramadhan Abugor, Lieutenant Colonel Mathiang Malual for information gathering. In those days, we banked on an extremely strategic secret source from within the army general headquarters operation room. A courageous sergeant from Western Sudan, who declined to give us his actual name and was doing that for his security, decided to do what he did for what he had heard John Garang was saying about Sudan over Radio SPLA. That source delivered to us a reliable piece of information about the movement of forces throughout the war zone and other areas where they had been recently deployed.

Soon afterwards, one of our confidential sources had given us the file containing the government spending or "operational budget" as it was known of the Sudan Army, which we hurriedly sent to Garang before his meeting with the prime minister of Sudan, Sadiq Mahdi in Addis Ababa. To avoid the attention of the media and other curiosity seekers, the Ethiopian authorities prepared the venue of the meeting of the leading Sudanese protagonists, the prime minister and the rebel leader, in an impoverished suburb on the edge of the capital Addis Ababa. The building where the meeting took place was an equally modest house, probably the facility was used by the Ethiopian secret agents.

The SPLM/A delegation included John Garang and members of the movement's top leadership that included William Nyuon Bany, Arok Thon Arok and Yousif Kuwa Mekki.

Captain Atem Yaak Atem who was then the director of Radio SPLA, was there to cover the meeting. He told me that when Sadiq el Mahdi arrived for the meeting, he positioned himself to capture Garang the Prime Minister of Sudan greeting each other. But that was not going to happen. He told me that when the two men were approaching each other, possible for an embrace, a common Sudanese practice, Sadiq raised his hands, signalling that he didn't want the occasion to be photographed. Out of courtesy, Garang waved Atem off. He complied and left the room for the meeting to begin. No photos of that meeting were ever taken because Sadiq el Mahdi didn't want to be seen cozying up with a man his constituency considered an outlaw.

In the first week of May 1983, we, a group of 53 citizens from Abyei, were finally released from detention in Khartoum after three months. We were suspected of leading the Anya Nya Two, whom Khartoum, accused of slaughtering a dozen Northern merchants in Ariath. In those days our committee in Khartoum received an elaborate message from Garang, requesting us to recruit comrades from the Nuba Mountains, Darfur and Blue Nile. That message coincided with my going to Abyei and to Kadugli, to visit our relatives living there. I was excited to know that Edward Ayong Soli was in Abyei and through him I met the leader of our Abyei Resistance Army, Miakol Deng Kuol and gave him the message about the birth of the movement and appealed to him to join the new movement. Edward Ayong, after that meeting, accompanied us to Kadugli.

In Kadugli, we stumbled on Yousif Kuwa Mekki, a schoolteacher, who was from the Nuba Mountains.

During the secret meeting I conveyed to him that *A progressive movement has been born, open to all the Sudanese. The Sudan*

People's Liberation Movement with a military wing, the Sudan People's Liberation Army, under the leadership of Dr John Garang de Mabior. He is a PhD holder, a Dinka from Bor and a colonel in the Sudanese army heading the military research unit and a lecturer at the University of Khartoum, Faculty of Agriculture. Although Dr John Garang does not know you in person, he has sent me to ask you to join him in the struggle. He has heard about you from other colleagues and from me. He would like you to join hands with him and the rest of his colleagues to liberate Sudan. Please, think of that and let me know whenever ready. Thanks. Soon afterwards we left for our separate destinations.

It took Yousif Kuwa Mekki three months before he came to meet me with the other comrades in September 1983 in Khartoum. He was accompanied by Abdel Aziz Adam Hilu, whom he introduced to me as one of his strong comrades within the Kumolo Youth organisation, leading resistance in the Nuba Mountains. Abdel Aziz Adam Hilu was also ready to join the movement. Yousif Kuwa had agreed, and we requested from the SPLM/A office in Addis Ababa for his tickets from Addis to be followed by his wife and children. I had the ticket for Yousif Kuwa Mekki on me when I was out to visit my daughter, Vilma, who had undergone an operation in a hospital and then to see Yousif that same evening.

There and then, as I was crossing a street I was shadowed and arrested by security operatives, who first took me home for further search. I was very lucky to be home again, where I had the opportunity to furtively pass the ticket in an envelope to my sister, Helen Achol, who was standing close behind me. They collected my brother-in-law, Donato Deng Mayen and I was taken to a detention centre where we met Mustafa Biong, who was also under arrest. Achol hid the envelope and passed it to Peter Nyot. Nyot eventually sent the ticket covertly to Yousif Kuwa, who left for Addis Ababa without delay. To avoid suspicion, his ticket was Khartoum-Cairo route instead of the shorter Khartoum-Addis Ababa alternative.

In April 1984, Dr Justin Yach arrived in Khartoum from Wau, tired of the way things were running, prepared to join the movement. As we were arranging for his departure through Nairobi, the Vice President General Joseph Lagu conveyed his disappointment with some elders in the movement who showed their opposition to Garang for his leadership style and talked about changing him. General Joseph Lagu sent an urgent and top-secret letter to the Ethiopian leader Lieutenant Colonel Mengistu Haile Mariam, about that development.

In fact, Vice President Lagu had intended to convey that vital communication to the head of the Ethiopian government about the intention of the Chief of Intelligence of Sudan, Omer Mohamed Tayeb (who was also the country's First Vice) to assassinate John Garang, involving some Ethiopians. General Joseph Lagu decided to convey the message about the plot to Mengistu. Yach discussed it with Lieutenant Colonel Mathiang Malual, who informed us. We agreed with sending the message. Such a letter would amount to recognising what the Ethiopian leader was doing to help our people. That message by Lagu was interpreted as an explicit endorsement of the rebellion against the government. Although the stand was an obvious contradiction, it was a moral boost to the movement.

That specific matter concerning Vice President Joesph Lagu was left for Lieutenant Colonel Mathiang Malual and me to handle. We informed our Ethiopian friends about the importance of such a serious message from a vice president of Sudan. They sent for their Minister of the Interior who was on his way to Libya, to pass by Khartoum on his way back to Addis Ababa. We looked for the safest place to host the meeting. Mathiang Malual talked to Justin Yach, being his friend. Yach accepted to host the meeting and I joined them after finding a safe place, where we discussed the issue. We were happy that we were in a position to contribute towards averting a plot that was going to hurt the inchoate liberation movement.

At Erkawit, a suburb in southern Khartoum, Bona Malwal Madut had a house, but the National Security had detained him at that time. Only Dr Justin Yach Arop had access to the house as a relative and no other person. My role was to lead Ismail and our guest to the house after providing beverages. Mathiang Malual was to bring General Joseph Lagu, while Justin Yach was to keep his eyes wide open in and around the house. When the time approached at 07:30 in the evening, the three men met: Joseph Lagu, the Ethiopian minister for the interior and the consul general of Ethiopia, Ismail Hassan. They met for about two hours.

In that meeting Lagu wrote his letter to Colonel Mengistu Haile Mariam of Ethiopia, in confidence, thanking him and his government for receiving his Southern Sudanese people, the movement and Garang personally and conveyed to Colonel Mengistu Haile Mariam the plan Khartoum was brooding to eliminate Garang. And he requested him to protect and take good care of Garang and not to allow the former "confused politicians" to destroy the movement. He added that Garang was a qualified officer of high calibre, and he knew him since the days they were both in the bush. Both the minister and consul Ismail became happy, and they took the letter the following day to Addis. That letter helped the movement in many ways and demonstrated to our friends the Ethiopians, how our people were united behind the SPLM/A and John Garang, from the vice president downwards. Which meant that, the future of the people of Southern Sudan was connected to the SPLM/A under Garang. That Khartoum's cell was a beehive of activity.

10

The SPLM/SPLA's Birth Pangs

No person in the movement can claim that there was a leader who fixed a specific date for SPLM/A to be born. May 16, 1983, was not the zero hour. That day was chosen for being an eventful day for the revolution to be born for the breaking of the gates of hell in Bor, to do what people wanted, as happened at Gore in July 1983. No person fixed the date in which our liberation struggle was to start. For instance, it could have been any day within that month or another day in a different month. However, May 16, 1983, marked the beginning of the armed confrontation that later evolved into full-scale warfare between the SPLA and the Sudan Armed forces (SAF), an armed conflict, unlike the mutinies in Juba in 1974 and 1975 or the Akobo revolt of March 1975. The fighting that erupted at Malual Chaat, a few kilometres away from Bor town, was an event that would, in the words of John Garang during his arrival in Khartoum in 2005, change Sudan forever.

Publicly, and throughout Southern Sudan, people did not know much about the rise of a political organisation known as National Liberation Movement in Bor. The town's inhabitants were hearing guns being fired but made little of what was happening. Some could remember previous unsuccessful mutinies at Juba airport in 1976, Akobo military garrison in 1975, Kapoeta army garrison in 1976, the tragic encounter between Captain Aguet and Brigadier Emmanuel Abur Nhial in Wau 1976, the Anya Nya II in Bentiu in 1978, Abyei Resistance in 1980 and Anya Nya Two in Ariath in 1983. During those years, Southern Sudan was experiencing—since 1972, the year when the Addis Ababa Agreement came into being in March—some instability created by such isolated armed confrontation between elements from the former Anya Nya fighters and members of the Sudan Armed Forces.

There were small uprisings, which occurred throughout Southern Sudan. Our people were displeased and supplicated for the coming of a new dawn in which confrontation would explode to free all the people from the yoke of subjugation.

The belief to liberate ourselves started to spread and became fixed in every mind and heart of many Southern Sudanese. Frequent armed confrontations were seen as an expression of dissent against the system of rule based in Khartoum, but nearly all of them fizzled out within days of their flare-ups. However, the events that occurred in Bor on May 16, 1983 inside the barracks at Malual Chaat, a few kilometres southeast of Bor town because of an issue which arose within the army connected to the "delayed salaries", turned out to be the exception. The mutiny was the beginning of the rebellion that led to the birth of the SPLM/A, a political-military body in years that followed changed Sudan in a way that nobody, including the very masterminds of the mutiny, had even imagined.

At the time there was general discontent within Southern Sudan among the Anya Nya forces whose members, particularly in Equatoria, were complaining about the way the Addis Ababa Agreement was being implemented, which was ignited by the transfer of forces to the North. The leader of the protest was unknown for some time. What that explosion in Bor was called, no person knew.

There were news reports being whispered about "a certain Major Kerubino Kuanyin Bol from Bahr el Ghazal", who fired the first bullet to signal the battle in which he was wounded in the shoulder.

People in and around Bor began to feel danger approaching. Hence, they decided to leave the town and hunt for other safer places when the army was determined to do something more than protest the delay of the salaries for the army. At that time, a group of elites emerged and engaged themselves in getting money from the merchants for the army. They attempted to dissuade the army from causing havoc, but to return to the barracks and keep Bor at peace. But things fell ascender. Those handy elite hardly captured what that shooting was all about. They assumed what flared up in Bor was a sort of protest in the barracks for delayed salaries and things would be normal once the army was paid, as was the case in other districts.

As people deserted Bor town in large numbers, the elite began to sense the danger coming and saw cattle herders, the peasants, leading the exodus, trekking towards Ethiopia, where people regrouped and waited for eventualities, as they began to organise. To hike from many parts of Southern Sudan was so difficult an idea to swallow, to many of our elite! Indeed, that was the hardest of all times in the entire history of the rise of the movement, during which need haunted every person. Everything was lacking, from means of livelihood to leadership.

People heard about leaders who had gone ahead, among them, Samuel Gai Tut, William Abdalla Chuol, Akuot Atem and those who proceeded far towards Boma hills. Some lined up behind men from their ethnic groups, contrary to what was initially agreed in Juba that, Samuel Gai Tut was to go and prepare the ground for Benjamin Bol Akok, the chairman of the National Action Movement, (NAM) since November 1979, in the house of Costa Lual Secondo in Juba Commercial Secondary School. In that capacity, Benjamin Bol, was to join them from London. Before William Abdalla Chuol, Akuot

Atem and especially Garang, would join them, being the person who had been chosen in Juba since 1982, to be the chief of staff of National Action Movement Liberation Army, NAMLA. That unfortunate confusion threatened to reverse the gains we had made so far.

Confusion arose and those who went ahead were bewildered beyond redemption and began to hunt for one another. Each of them headed his own way searching for leadership, on the verge of plunging into anarchy. Between those scattered pillars people were confused, each fighting for a favoured leader. But they were all related to NAM before each of them embarked on choosing a name for his own organisation. After the force in Ayod commanded by Captain William Nyuon rebelled, the units in Pochalla and Pibor in addition to defections from Malakal and other garrisons followed suit.

And people understood what was going on and they were happy. There were some insignificant insurgencies that merged into the movement with the arrival of people from Bahr el Ghazal and the Nuba Mountains, who joined those who met at Gore in July 1983 and formed the Sudan People's Liberation Movement and the Sudan People's Liberation Army. Almost all the people who crossed into Ethiopia were in fact, looking for a military solution rather than a political way to solve the problem. That fact, beside tribal inclinations of most of the lower segments of the recruits who joined the struggle, almost hampered the progress of the movement. But Garang and colleagues did their best, trying to address that issue over the years.

Earlier in Bor, beside the fortunate few who had access to long-range contact like the Jonglei Project in Bor and Panyagoor, the rest were all confused. Not one of them knew what was happening, except for a few who were in direct contact with Khartoum. Through the director of Jonglei Project, the late Daniel Deng Yong, we were present from behind the Sudanese intelligence. We received the news of whatever was happening in the area on time. That nature of secrecy gave chance to people without contacts to pause their presence and contribution in the creation of SPLM/A. Up to that time most of the people who had sacrificed for the movement had not spoken about their contributions until they passed away.

There was lots of confusion and people were divided between truth and illusion, about the real condition of that child born in that most difficult situation and whom should we call the new baby. It was one of the most capturing moments for a person to find themselves in, for the first time struggling in isolation. Those were moments in which a person would discover himself facing an event like the crossing of the last round in a grand tournament.

There were other reasons for that confusion. Most important of those was lack of accurate means of communication to help people visualise what was running, to cool down between the rapid flow of news from the field. That was where people got lost when they failed to find accurate means of information. Added to that, the nature of the news people were running after. As news kept on coming after that attack on Malual Gahoth in 1983, a lot of fabrications began to spread of fake heroism of their sons and the sophisticated weapons used by those who fired the first bullets during the first attack.

Despite all that, events were moving fast in a tense situation, where we could not raise our angry supporters from Southern Sudan to demonstrate in Khartoum. The military nature of the junta and the lack of a force to protect the rebellion, would have been a new thing to both Northern and Southern people in Khartoum. That move would have changed the nature of our struggle and put the army to face a new experience to confront people unlike Southern Sudanese rebels. People would have been scared by the novelty of that experience, which they had never tried before, when the confrontation turned into bloody military conflict between unarmed civilians and a full-fledged army. Hence, we had to be careful. That was the time the Sudanese people started to hear from the leaders of the *intifada*, the unavoidability of an armed force to protect civilians, if they were to confront a maddened junta.

One fundamental fact, which drew our attention was how could a popular national movement born among peasants grow and triumph as it emerged to converge into one broad-based national call by all the participants wherever, though in different ways. A liberation entity arising out of a society with a low political consciousness such as ours, surprisingly attracted a following from diverse communities and social classes for various reasons. This is what happened in 1983, when the insurgency was embraced even by the rural communities, cattle herders, students, workers and civil servants.

Primarily, a peasant-based insurgency is like a fast-flowing river that uproots and carries along anything in its path—shrubs, floating weeds, trees, animals—which it carries downstream. In the early days of the SPLM/A, the situation in Southern Sudan could be equated with that of a flowing river. Estimates of the war victims vary, but it is reckoned over two million people were either killed in the war or lost their lives due to war-related circumstances, and unknown numbers of people who had lost limbs or received various forms of disabilities. Despite those stunning losses our people went through, they never considered even for a minute to give up the struggle to end the oppression they were determined to end once and for all.

11

Charting a Revolutionary Roadmap

What people should know is that the rise of the movement was not a simple joke. In fact, the revolution began to make waves among the people individually, who were subjected to harsh oppression. Without organising the people intellectually for lacking capacity to confront oppression, there were many variations in the depth of intellectual and tactical ways in which the Southern Sudanese people's explosive anger, which was planted through turbulent centuries, attracted them into a living resistance that triumphed.

The process of building a formidable frontage to protect and revamp our march, especially during peace times, has not been given its deserved chance to grow and become a powerful one. Many things were left for another day and our people paid no attention until Garang appeared. There were many hindrances, which obstructed our march, for we paid no attention to ourselves to sense our problems from the roots, and where do we intended to go.

When confusion broke out, no person knew or bothered to follow the real nature of the shooting in Bor and how it developed and who was the real leader. Sergeant Yousif Kiir, who considered himself the leader of the rebellion in Bor, asserted himself as the leader of

"Southern Sudan Liberation Movement", supported by Samuel Gai Tut. To which Garang objected, in the few days in which they were in Thiajak, before the helicopter arrived. Our people clearly saw things unfolding. They saw lawlessness dominating the towns behind them and that was all. Which was not a normal situation in which to sit and wait for a leader whose days of coming were unknown, while tension and anguish were growing in that barren hopelessness. People went ahead to look for a leader to usher them out of that intensifying darkness.

The clear indicator of who the leader would be, was the arrival of a helicopter, which picked Garang out of other leaders in Thiajak on the Sudanese-Ethiopian border on June 13, 1983, with Captain Salva Kiir, Akuot Atem, and Samuel Gai Tut. Kiir left Malakal during the same time that Garang had withdrawn from Bor towards the Ethiopian border. The two rebelling officers met at Thiajak before the helicopter could arrive. Garang came well prepared with an elaborate unifying political and military program to start with, amidst confusion. From Thiajak, Garang was lifted to Gambela by General Mesfin, the Chief of Staff of the Ethiopian army, accompanied by Thokwath Pal, Party Secretary for Gambela Region.

The next day, June 14, they returned to Thiajak to lift the family of Garang to Itang. After a few days in Itang, Garang was taken to Colonel Mengistu Haile Mariam in Addis Ababa, during the third week of June 1983. And after meeting Mengistu in Addis Ababa, Garang went ahead to organise a historic conference for the people who were at Itang. The meeting was held at Gore, an old town on high land east of Gambela, in early July 1983 to decide and agree on:

- the name for the organisation
- the name for the military wing
- the design of an emblem for the movement
- writing and approval of a manifesto spelling out the objectives of the movement and the means for achieving them, and

- the election of the leadership to guide and direct the political and military struggle. And there, Colonel Dr John Garang was elected to become chairman of the Sudan People's Liberation Movement (SPLM) and commander in chief of the Sudan People's Liberation Army (SPLA).

At that stage in the history of the SPLA, Garang began to seriously embark on building a qualitative force. And he elaborately spoke about that on many occasions. Addressing his forces in Hamish Koreib in Eastern Sudan as he had on several occasions before, Garang thanked the forces, saying that they were the real New Sudan forces. He told them that he was happy with them, because they respected civilians and protected their belongings. And that is how a freedom fighter should always be, to look at the cause people wanted to achieve. But our people were still behind what they should have known, to make them realise what route to take to liberate themselves. The road to liberation was still incomplete. Most of the people felt deep pains of the loss of Garang at a time when the contemptuous began to celebrate, lauding anti-Garang slogans, without attending to what they mean to demonstrate to others.

Shortly after Garang's premature and widely lamented departure, there were people who opted to erase his shining achievements and his illustrious legacy. As if that insult was not bad enough, his detractors who went to dub all the citizens who followed Garang's objectives and methods had to be vilified by calling them "*awalaad Garang*", which in Arabic means "Garang's boys", not a complimentary label, but a disparaging classification by those who despised everything Garang stood for as well as the achievements of the SPLM/A under his able command.

We cannot begin to deny our history. As lofty objects, monuments are hard to complete by their initiators. Monuments take a long time and creativity to build. But people would always be there, though few, to finish the good job begun by the great minds who initiated them. Garang succeeded to build a strong army, but not the exemplary one he envisioned. He planned to form a new progressive party, but confronted many hurdles, which need us to complete forming, though building a democratic people's party has no specific time within which to be accomplished.

Right from Gore, Garang sent a message that assigned Dr Lam Akol Ajawin to take charge of the movement's Khartoum office (secret cell). I was designated to assist Lam with intelligence activities until the time he left for the headquarters. I remained to steer the boat of intelligence assisted by Peter Kok, James Yuang Anyieth, Ramadhan Abugor and others until I left Khartoum for the bush on May 28, 1987, when the Umma Party decided to take me for my "Last Supper". Garang avoided mudslinging, in which the other leaders got stuck to the extent of exchanging fire among themselves. Garang went ahead to organise the movement. The congress established the political wing, SPLM and the army the SPLA from different groups and trades on sound organisational and political principals.

Our people should reflect and coolly examine whether Garang intentionally delayed the building of a strong political vanguard to lead our liberation movement or not. They should also examine what Garang really stood for. The man might have unintentionally committed mistakes like any person, looking at the intricate nature of responsibilities bestowed upon him by destiny. His mistakes might have been seen through the eyes of a person who looked at him from a subjective angle. But as he left us, we should be able to fill any gap to protect, develop and block diverters from hijacking the movement. And the protection of the movement can only be achieved when all the members are politically enlightened and socially sound, as envisaged by Garang.

In every field, Garang made an example to be followed. He cleared the land, dug the soil and planted different varieties of seeds. He did not plant in the desert. He was aware of the apathy which might confront his people and began to remove it from their way. He stressed the point of carefulness and vigilance to every group trained. Garang was much concerned about the future of the movement and its protection from being hijacked by opportunists. Unfortunately, Garang did not live long to tend to what he planted and see it germinate, grow, flower and fruit. So, development is a demanding process, which might take human lives. But those who inherited Garang behaved as if they had been told to chop off the very branch on which they were seated.

Now that our destiny was about to drown in confusion, which might lead our people to more fragmentations, where next do we go? And if not, what should people do in a tense situation, where the movement, and not those running and managing it, were being held responsible for the misfortunes, which caused the pains and wounds in our hearts. The only thing to point at was the fact that our people were compelled to feel and see the movement's shortcomings through the eyes of a people who were begging for survival, during the war and suddenly rose during peace times to grab gold through crooked means. Some people took the movement as a provider of jobs for the needy and accumulate wealth for the greedy. That was where we intentionally missed the road inaugurated by Garang.

Our people were being misled, in questioning the realities of the time. How could a movement such as the SPLM/A, which led the people for 22 years, turn against those it liberated in such an inhumane way, in a matter of three years? How can a movement, which confronted tribalism for more than twenty years, begin to preach and kill people based on their ethnic or regional affiliations. There are people who refuse to admit mistakes committed by their relatives, friends and colleagues. However, in the context of bodies such as liberation movements, mistakes committed by their leaders should not be judged as personal, but rather on the organisations in whose names credits, responsibility or guilt should be apportioned.

Unless people review all those ways, we shall never make it, in a situation in which people live in fear. Yes, destroy South Sudan as a new nation, but where would people go when children are forced to discontinue education now, because they lack the means to continue learning? It is shameful that people are getting lost between instant gains for which they have been incited to kill one another, and all the sacrifices we made with grave mistakes, since people began to think otherwise. Between 1983 and 1994, people under Garang were following the right track after many years of oppression. But unfortunately, because of ignorance covered with greed.

Unless there is a means by which people could understand the power play inherent in a liberation struggle, we would not have made it. There was a need to identify the elements that contributed to the success of our liberation at all stages, which led the people to move forward. In our case, whatever was accomplished by SPLM was not the work of one person, nor did it fall from heaven. In any organisation formed there were cadres leading it. But this stopped short when their intellectual and organisational capabilities turned into apathy, when they failed to move forward, like a truck loaded for a specific destination running out of fuel somewhere in a wilderness.

That is the reason SPLM/A, as a broad-based people's movement, moved like a great river flowing from where several tributaries converge. Within its ranks, contrast and variety were to be found in abundance: the upright and crooks; old and young; tall and short, from different trades and ways of life; scholars and unschooled; humorous and prim, and so forth. Being the outcome of every sacrifice people made during the liberation, their reward was constantly coping with hardships and sometimes death. Yet despite all that, their opponents branded the freedom fighters with labels which were contrary to the noble cause they had dedicated their lives to achieve.

Speaking about the role of the revolutionaries, John Garang once said, "We all converged in this movement from different walks of life. We should therefore get organised to move together to the end of the march." But after John Garang left, we stopped. Under the circumstance, it was imperative to ask, "When will we move to liberate ourselves?"

May 16, 1983, became a symbolic day. There were other anti-government movements all over Southern Sudan in the liking of that great resistant one, which was born in Torit in 1955. Born skinny, fed with porridge, to use a South Sudanese idiom, but resisted until it mutated to Anya Nya and subsequently Anya Nya II, and finally to the emergence of the SPLM/A, as a mature movement. Our people need to know how they were interrelated.

Today along the main streets of Juba, for instance and in many circles, many are astonished to see and read names of people being raised to the level of sainthood for the negative parts they played during the struggle, when they were in fact "betrayers of the people". That is the reason why words like deceitfulness, swindler, treason, thieves and misuse of politicised tribal traditions have totally lost their meanings in a South Sudanese dictionary in an unfortunate way, where plunderers of public resources became rich and began to consider themselves as celebrities. All those misguided trends were what Garang fought against until his death.

12

From a Modest Beginning to National Stewardship

John Garang de Mabior began his carrier as an army officer in Anya Nya and continued to confront all the pains, wounds and other forms of suffering which were the lot of all freedom fighters. There is no doubt about Garang's attributes as a highly intelligent and observant person, who could read human faces with diligence and who took appropriate notes of the faces he saw. Garang had a remarkable IQ (intelligence quotient), which could explain his success as an outstanding tactician, which neatly tied with his determination to persevere in the face of all manner of setbacks that are always to be encountered in a long and bitter armed and political struggle against a well-armed adversary, the government of Sudan, which was allied with some self-serving Southern Sudanese. Despite setbacks and reversals, which were common and expected, Garang never lost hope; instead, he was convinced that victory would be achieved no matter how long this would take. To be consistent with whatever he did was how he grew. He once told me over a phone, when I was in Washington, about what happened in our Blue Nile Axis, in December 1989. He assured me, "Yes, but one must have more than a way to resolve a problem. We are at war, you know." And he did that practically on many occasions, when his opponents in our ranks forgot about the war we were in, concentrating on trying to get rid of Garang.

The Sudanese Army, on one of its worst attacks ever against the movement, took over Kurmuk from the SPLA and overran Assosa and Tsore, Longkuei refugee camp, over eighty kilometres inside Ethiopia, supported by the Ethiopian People's Liberation Front (EPLF) from November to December 1989. Garang keenly followed the upsetting news about the losses we had incurred. He considered that to be "one of the greatest trying developments yet", he had to deal with, and which led his comrades on an unexpected route across the White Nile.

From there, he commanded the capture of Kajo Keji, destroyed Isaiah Paul's forces, captured Kaya, overran Morobo, attacked Yei after driving almost all the military vehicles out of the garrison, advanced on Lainya and threatened to attack Juba within a month.

On that matter he said, "You see, we should not lose initiative under any conditions. We just cannot afford that. We must always keep our morale higher than that of the enemy. If we fail to do so, then all our forces will be dejected and desert us. It has been said that 'an idle mind is a devil's workshop.' Is that not so?" That was what he told me after returning from that mission and I still could imagine him talking to me over phone until the moment I was writing these lines.

Garang taught me that the word "initiative" could mean little to some people who did not know how to get embroiled in the armed conflict. To achieve what is called element of surprise, which is fundamental in winning wars and thus, is critical in achieving victories. That was how the SPLM/A succeeded to maintain close friends like Ethiopia, Uganda and other friendly countries and entities, who opted to watch and monitor us remotely, but on our side, in a long-protracted war where no victor was so simple to predict between the SPLM/A and the totalitarian governments of the Sudan; in which we were noted to be victorious. He said, "Once a state gets tied to a peg called stalemate, then its days are numbered."

Garang added that, "All the cutting-edge tactics are essentially lifeblood of guerilla warfare based on creating and planting constant fear in the enemy."

To maintain the initiative according to the logic of guerilla warfare, is to constantly terrorise the enemy by hitting unexpected areas to incapacitate the enemy and ensure its defeat, as the saying goes. And that was an important weapon, which Garang maintained throughout the struggle. Kicking off from Kajo Keji, Kaya, Morobo, Yei to Lainya and successively frightening Juba, was what the SPLA did in the field along the way to Juba. It terrorised the enemy in Juba. Despite the distance and huge numbers of forces, which were there, they feared to come out of Juba.

That spirited and sustained attack on Juba in June 1992, had made the Sudan Armed Force (SAF) panic when they found themselves out of the trenches and on the verge of total incapacitation. Confusion gripped the government forces who began to exchange fire among themselves, as fire was hitting them virtually from every direction. Frightened by an enemy they were unable to see, but felt around them for the first time in the history of war in Southern Sudan. Had the main pieces of SPLA artillery not stuck in the mud at Khor Ramla to the south of the town by then, Juba was on the verge of falling to the SPLA during the first week of June 1992. Despite the bitter fact that those of Cdr Riek Machar and Cdr Lam Akol stood to pin down the forces we had mobilised from coming to Juba in their calculation that if Juba fell to the forces under Garang's command, that would have signalled the end of their agenda—toppling and replacing him—of those who were preparing to stab us in the back and spell an end to their relevance in the struggle. Because of those types of moves, myopic individuals who failed to score victories would be ready to sabotage the agenda of their rivals, a sad statement about competitiveness and power struggle, which is unfortunately common in Africa even among rivals who share a common enemy.

In fact, the capture of Kajo Keji and the threat to Juba, were such distressing developments for the Sudan government that they didn't even expect such would ever happen. But what made the difference was the fact that Kajo Keji, Kaya, Morobo and Yei were as far south of Southern Sudan as Kurmuk is from Khartoum. The interpretation of this is that the further the wound from the heart, the lesser the danger is to the central authority in the twisted thinking of the sectarian rulers of Sudan living in the comfort of Khartoum the capital. All the difficulties being faced by the inhabitants of the peripheries have never been the concern of the governing authorities. But when the news reached people in the refugee camps in Dima, Itang and Pinywudo, the refugees publicly celebrated the victories scored by the gallant and unpaid SPLA fighters. Despite the celebration of military victories, they knew in nearly all the battles the SPLA engaged with the SAF, there were fallen heroes. For that reason, the understanding has always been that a liberation movement must be dedicated to the cause of the people, courageous, and its members to undertake all steps which would lead to the achievement of the overall goal of the liberation: freedom, justice for all and the unity of the people, goals of the SPLM/A as clearly articulated by John Garang.

That swift and accurate move erased all the sadness, which the enemy plastered on our faces by the loss of innocent lives, the taking of Kurmuk and destruction of Tsore and Longkuei refugee camps at the border with Ethiopia.

But adversaries within our ranks believed that the role of Garang had finished as a leader of the movement with the tragic loss of Kurmuk and Tsore, to which they had no solution. They did not even try to console the people for their losses. But Garang set and waited for the most appropriate chance to move. He moved quietly, but swiftly, however long that took him. He was never shaken by defeat, because Garang would be diligently prepared to confront the enemy whenever, wherever they came from. He looked carefully for an alternative route and moved accordingly, maintaining the initiative.

After hitting the enemy, he returned to Pinywudo and went to Itang to console the people for the bitter losses. Garang was never shaken by the loss of a battle but concentrated on the outcome of the war. The most important thing for him was not to lose the initiative. The war Garang was commanding took him twenty-two years, facing the Sudan Armed Forces (SAF), which was equipped with superior arms supplied mostly by the Arab world and the countries of Eastern Europe, when Nimeiri was singing Marxist-Leninist slogans.

After parting company with the countries of the Soviet bloc following the abortive coup that was masterminded by his former colleagues and pro-Moscow colleagues in July 1971, Nimeiri made an about-turn to embrace the US camp, which initially believed his claim that he was fighting an insurgency that was communist inspired. Despite all that, the SPLA frequently replenished their armoury with the weapons that they captured in battles with SAF, hence making Nimeiri the movement's quartermaster in Garang's words. In that balance of power, Garang never doubted that Khartoum was not going to crush the SPLA and then dictate the government's terms on a militarily weak movement at a negotiating table. That judgement later proved to be correct. Since the time of the peace talks between the Government of Sudan and the SPLM/A from the late 1990s to 2005, the dialogue was more of equals talking virtually on equal terms. Garang signed the Comprehensive Peace Agreement (CPA) of February 2005 on behalf of the movement, fully convinced that it was a just peace agreement to meet the aspirations of the people.

13

A New Dimension to Politics

John Garang never disliked something or anybody for nothing. Even if he did not tell you the reason, one would come to know at depth later when, for instance, he refused to be interviewed by Ishaq Ahmed Fadlallah of *Al Intibaha* newspaper, an organ for the Islamist groupings. Garang came to know that Ishaq intended to sit with him and take exposures, with the intention to use them in his own way to create more fears in Khartoum about Dr Garang, contrary to what the media would say.

Almost all the media of the world converged in Naivasha and Nairobi to interview Garang, at the time of the signing of the Comprehensive Peace Agreement (CPA). Almost every journalist who attended that historic occasion, had a chance to interview Garang except for Ishaq Ahmed Fadlallah. He told me, "No, please, not Ishaq in particular." I was so surprised. Why would Garang refuse to be interviewed by such an important Islamic fundamentalist journalist with whom we were on the verge of concluding an historic agreement?

But as time went on, I came to fully understand the reason why Garang refused to be interviewed by Ishaq Ahmed Fadlallah in person. Simply, because Ishaq Ahmed Fadlallah, whom I had the bad luck to meet face to face in an open arena for the second time in The Hague, the Dutch capital city, was a mischievous character. He was an ardent misfit who hated himself for his unappealing physical outlook, compounded by the awkward way he carried himself, and his incomprehensible manner of communication. Ishaq deluded himself that he was intelligent, brave and an intellectual despite his crude use of language and blatant belligerence. For his part, Garang did not accept to be humiliated by such a character that was the epitome of what could be objectionable in a public figure.

Garang loved clear, intelligent, forthright thinking, dignified and humble people. He was careful to deal with crooks, the deceitful and the lazy. In his first meeting with Prime Minister Sadiq Abdel Rahman al Mahdi in Addis Ababa, the two gentlemen held a marathon talk, lasting over eight hours and Sadiq Mahdi told Garang to put it in the communiqué that they had only met for less than two hours. Garang told him that was not correct. It would be false not to tell people the truth. Garang stated, "We cannot start by telling our people something far from the truth. Why not tell them we met for eight hours?" The prime minister said nothing, embarrassed by what he had attempted to say. He was astonished by what Garang had told him, and he left the meeting place totally confused. He never expected a Southern Sudanese to address him in that tough way, as a privileged member of the Mahdi family as he believed.

Garang favoured ideas which were relevant and capable of being applied to a given situation, He avoided squandering his time and energy on nonessential things. For instance, in a confusing moment when a person could be swayed to forget something within reach and desperately start to search for it, they could be confronted by a greater provocation: someone could be standing in the middle of a fresh running stream and ask his comrades where to quench his thirst. Garang would be the person to tell that bewildered fellow: "Oh, so you want to drink now? What about the water you are standing in?" His presence was felt wherever he was, especially in the battlefield where the news of his presence or arrival at any place would spread waves of euphoria.

John Garang shrewdly grasped how to weigh and tackle problems according to their importance and urgency in a simple way. To him, things must have a meaning, to convince people to handle them accordingly. In the battle for Torit in 1989, two of our combatants found a small bottle of liquid in the hospital's theatre. They took the bottle, thinking it was water and were preparing to drink. Despite the warning by their comrades, the two gulped the chemical, which was anaesthetic. They soon collapsed and died there and then. When Garang was informed of the tragedy, he became sorry for such a pointless loss.

****

Garang was intensely reviled by some individuals within his country and outside. Such hatred and opposition could be likened to the way the prophets of ancient times were reviled or even killed by their own people. Such rejection always stems from either ignorance of the message, or jealousy. Based on the understanding that "familiarity breeds contempt", messengers, whether in the spiritual or political domain, are sometimes rejected by their own people. They simply cannot believe that one of their own could attract a crowd or a whole nation, who embrace and believe in the worth of the message such leaders articulate.

They would prefer to sacrifice for the continuation of an archaic order, which they understand and manipulate to benefit them. Some individuals went as far as imploring the divine being to take Garang away. Strange enough, when he died in a helicopter crash, those critics deluded that God had answered their prayers. Certainly,

Garang left in a way that was described as mysterious as they still raise hard questions. Numerous theories have been advanced concerning Garang's departure, and more are being created with the intention to tarnish or erase the legacy he truly deserves. All those attempts can only give us lessons about life and how we should relate to one another, as fallible beings.

The cardinal fact that Garang was killed when the helicopter's rear left wheel hit a solid rock and the aircraft suddenly rolled on top of the mountain in bad weather, became conclusive. But it was not accepted that an accident was the cause of the death of all those who were with him on board. Had the investigators examined the way the helicopter was flown in that tribulation without any human error? Garang was the only person those individuals expected to die in that way. Many people were even confused and refused to believe other probabilities in which similar tragedies happen and began to think of other theories without examining what really happened, such as the fact that the helicopter rolled six times and exploded on top of the mountain. For them, the most important thing was that Garang died in that way, though people at large wished him to have lived much longer to bring the mission to its logical conclusion: attainment of freedom with justice.

So, our supplication to heaven should be taken as a normal human wish, as to why he was taken at that time, when he still had critical things to accomplish. During the burial of Dr John Garang de Mabior in Juba, I saw a contemptuous-looking elder pacing towards the graveside at the time when people were leaving after the interment. That character was seen smiling and sometimes laughing during the sombre atmosphere in which many people preferred to communicate in low and sad voices as they were leaving. But that individual could not hide his openly cheerful mood, which was judged to be on the side of hilarity by those who furtively watched the man's contented demeanour.

That character didn't even try to conceal his mien, an open book of happiness amidst the sombre crowd. None paid him attention because he went unnoticed. He stood for a few moments, stared and left, neither grief nor a dot of sorrow on his smooth relaxed face as he left the graveside. That character appeared—even booked a flight to Juba to be at the funeral to ascertain for himself that it was John Garang, who he hated with a passion, that was the one being buried and not someone else.

However, there were persons who hated Garang because he was the type of leader that would not settle for half-baked measures or flimsy ideas. One could not attempt to play with him. If he had wanted to enrich himself, for instance, he would not have picked up a gun and walked to the bush. Garang did not decide to resort to the bush like a tourist. Nor was there a person who could take him for a traditional power-hungry soldier with whom to connive. John Garang was academically and intellectually exposed more than they were. All those grumpy ones, who expressed their hatred in words and deeds, have come to fully realise how dangerous their deeds are today, for attempting to rob what belongs to other people, with tragedies facing them in their individual walks in life.

John Garang was a well-rounded person in matters related to military, political game and in the sphere of social relations. He was also an outstanding intellectual. These qualities necessarily qualified him to lead the movement then in the making. Until his death, he tried his best to increase his diverse knowledge about the Sudan. Garang was a distinguished scholar with a PhD in agricultural economics. He headed the research department of the Sudanese armed forces and lectured in the Faculty of Agriculture at the University of Khartoum, when he decided to join the liberation movement. In 1989 I happened to accompany him on a visit to his distinguished Professor Timmons at Iowa State University and we continued to his graduate college in Grinnell on a visit to Professor John Dawson who was exceptionally proud of him. Once graduated from Grinnell he had headed to Addis Ababa to closely follow talks then he proceeded to the bush, where he was trained and became a freedom fighter and was commissioned as a captain in the bush before his absorption as captain in the Sudan army.

Garang was absorbed into the Sudanese Army until he became a colonel, who was sent to attend a commanders' course at Fort Bunning, Georgia, in the USA, when he was a major and completed very successfully, scoring third position in the history of the college.

Socially, John Garang was married to Mama Rebecca Nyandeng on December 19, 1974, and a proud father of five children. He was never a polygamist.

Once an inquisitive Nigerian journalist asked John Garang in 1987: "Dr Garang, are you married?"

"Yes," he replied, "I am married to a beautiful wife, and we have four children. Would that do?" That journalist was silent.

Dr John Garang was an intellectual. He brought in new things into Sudanese politics like diagrams, Venn diagrams and charts, to illustrate his ideas and he studied the history of ancient Sudan, especially of the Nile Valley. To Garang, books were among his closest companions.

Garang took great interest in and studied the UNESCO-sponsored series on the history of Africa, UNESCO works of Professor Cheikh Anta Diop about African history and the Nile Valley, volume II in particular. When he visited Egypt, Garang gave an impressive lecture in the International Conference Hall, which was compiled into a book authored by Dr Wathig Kameir, a senior member of the movement. Garang visited the pyramids and other antiquities to learn firsthand of the rich past of Egypt, whose illustrious history is intimately linked to that of Sudan. During his stay in Egypt Garang visited the grave of Ali Abdel Latif, the Sudanese army officer of Southern origin, who masterminded the 1924 White Flag League mutiny in the Sudan, who was sentenced to prison and sent to Wau and later transferred to Cairo where he died in detention, which no Sudanese leader has ever done. Garang did the same to other martyrs of the later years and paid respect to the memory of William Deng Nhial, Victoria Yaar Arol and Captain Mathiang Gumwel in Tonj in 1997.

Garang's knowledge of the Sudanese political scene lifted him above many politicians, if not all. His long elaborate letter dated January 31, 2000, to Sadiq Mahdi, the former Sudanese prime minister, demonstrated his excellence. In his response, he logically and in a scholarly way analysed the history of the Umma Party from 1964 until today, holding it responsible for leading the adamant refusal of the previous governments to implement the resolutions pertaining to the contention of the civil war in the Sudan, known as the Southern Problem. The way he diagnosed the Umma Party's stand in Asmara in 1995 was foretelling about how the Umma was moving to betray not only the National Democratic Alliance (NDA) but also all the Sudanese people. He held the Umma Party responsible for opposing him, refusing to recognise his leadership of the opposition National Democratic Alliance (NDA). Being a Southern Sudanese, who happened to lead the majority force in the NDA, he adopted a surrender approach—under the pretext of reconciliation—with the regime led by the Islamic fundamentalist of the National Islamic Front (NIF) in Khartoum. Which was the final blow that sent Sadiq Mahdi out of the NDA to Khartoum.

There was not a single instance when Garang was ever accused of wrongdoing, such as embezzlement of public funds or being involved in acts that could tarnish his dignity and standing. He could not move to hold accountable those who enriched themselves during the war, without being reported for having done harm to the movement or individuals. Many officers and men were punished for proven crimes connected to unacceptable ways of self-enrichment or similar crimes in a situation where there was nothing much to swindle and no laws to apply and exact on perpetrators and culprits. The movement was simply guided by SPLM Penal and Disciplinary Laws, 1984 and customary laws based on commonsense, which could change from one place to the other, according to the standard of those applying the sentences. Many aspects of the law were left to good conscience. Many of those accused of having done wrong in the movement, turned their anger against John Garang.

Garang never tolerated people endowed with opportunistic ideals and dreams, though he was always ready to embrace them once they apologised. He had a great forgiving heart. Some of the people we see roving aimlessly today, who mastered the art of ambulating between friends and foes would acknowledge this fact. These are the kind of people who fly to apologise to masters in Khartoum and turn against their own people in the home of their birth. But we need not list their names, for that line would lead nowhere.

Garang believed that an oppressed person should not in turn become an oppressor as that would amount to hypocrisy and a contradiction in terms. And he demonstrated that when he stood firm in support of the rights of women, which he stated in his living quote:

Women are the marginalised of the marginalised people.

Garang stood by his word until it was implemented as demonstrated in the Interim Constitutions of States, South Sudan and the Government of National Unity of Sudan. In which women rights were indicated to be 25 per cent minimum of whatever we do at the time, which he considered to be the beginning of correcting the historical gender imbalances in this backward phase of development.

14

Meeting His Last Surviving Maternal Aunt

We left Maiwut after Pagak to Nasir and Ulang from January to March 1990, during the Bright Star Campaign. Commanders Riek Machar, Lam Akol, Gordon Kong, Stephen Dual and Vincent Kuany were with us when Garang joined us to begin the scheduled operations in Upper Nile Region. But things did not work the way we planned. There was another minor but vital mission that popped up almost out of the blue and had to be tackled instantly. The emergency was an advancing enemy military boat heading to Malakal from Kosti. As commander in chief of the SPLA, Garang had to give orders for military preparedness: reinforcement and rations from Renk sailing towards Jebel Mohammed Agha, with no road to use, only compass. That was a great target of chance. Had we succeeded to hit that steamer, it could have changed the whole course of the war and perhaps, changed the government in Khartoum. Garang assigned that mission to commanders Tahir Bior of engineer corps, James Hoth representing the intelligence unit (who hails from the area), and Rostum Ali Mustafa of the infantry. We were proceeding to Ulang.

We all departed Maiwut that same evening. Besides that, Cdr

Lam Akol Ajawin, A/Cdr Isaac Tut and A/Cdr Nhial Deng Nhial at Khor Yabus, launched a poorly coordinated attack on Yabus, which was unexpectedly repulsed by the enemy. Our forces heading for Kurmuk and forward towards Damazin front began to disperse, which negatively affected the whole campaign. In that attack Cdr Lam Akol was almost captured by the enemy, but was saved by some of his gallant comrades who pulled him out of that massive counterattack by the enemy from his tactical headquarters and dragged him out in a jeep with four flat tyres. Thank heavens, he was saved with all his comrades.

Despite that, Garang, who was the overall commander of the Bright Star Campaign, had to proceed from Nasir to Ulang to oversee our advance on Malakal before our forces under the command of Cdr Stephen Dual were to cross the Nile to Kodok. From Kodok northwards our forces were under Cdr Riek Machar. From Yabus to Kurmuk we were commanded by Cdr Lam and from Kurmuk to the north, commanded by Cdr Martin Manyiel Ayuel. That campaign was set to leave Cdr Gordon Kong around Malakal. Garang was escorted to Ulang by commanders Stephen Dual, Vincent Kuany, Tahir Bior, Oyay Deng, James Hoth, Gier Chuang, Mohammed Saeid Bazara, and me, among other officers of various ranks. We spent two weeks at Ulang. After our fourth day, John Garang received Cdr Salva Kiir arriving from Watt. On the other hand, Cdr Garang had sent scouts to Anakdiar—near Malakal—headed by Cdr Oyay, deputised by Cdr Gier Chuang.

Luckily, the enemy had no knowledge of the presence of our two commanders at Anakdiar. From there, they sent three Hino trucks loaded with sorghum, salt, biscuits and watches to Cdr Gordon Kong at Anakdiar, as a gesture for future cooperation in the process of his surrendering to government forces, supervised by the Governor of Upper Nile, Gatluak Deng in Malakal. Both Oyay and Gier decided to detain the trucks and not to let them return to Malakal, proceeding with them to Itang to be used by the movement.

Cdr Gordon Kong had to seal his mouth for having been discovered "selling the campaign strategy to the enemy", allegations that were communicated clandestinely but which some among us believed had some substance to them. I received the trucks at Ulang. Eventually we ordered them to transport about 250 small children who were sent from Bentiu walking all the way to Ethiopia for education in Itang refugee camp. Garang, however, later changed the plan to Tharpam and instructed Cdr Taban Deng, who was the coordinator for Itang refugee camp to execute the directives. On his way after two weeks from Ulang to Gambela, Garang stopped to see how the children were coping with the new conditions. He joined the children in all that they were doing at school: learning and playing.

At Ulang I was introduced to Dieu Gai, who was over 95 years of age. He had been a soldier since the British colonial days. Dieu had a lot of bizarre and amusing things around him. For instance, his chair was made of ceremonial "hyena hide", designed to scare dogs away. Across the Sobat River I was shown what remained of a cannibalised Land Rover, which had been used by Garang and his family when travelling from Bor but had broken down beyond use. When he was heading to Ethiopia in 1983 with his wife Rebecca Nyandeng and her children, they started their long walk towards the borders from here.

About five days after arriving at Ulang, Wang Chok took me aside under a tree and introduced me to an elderly lady with a smiling face. Her name was Gak, named after Garang's mother, Gang Malual Kuol. The name Gak took me aback for a moment, for it sounded like the name of Gak Malual Kuol, Garang's mother, who died when Garang was a young schoolboy. Then she talked to me in Nuer because she must have been told that I was the one to lead her to where her son was.

I was surprised, though I found myself asking Wang again, "You mean Gak Malual Kuol, Garang's mother or what do you mean?"

"Yes, the sister of Garang's mother, the youngest sister," he answered, adding, "She was the aunt who took care of him after his mother had passed away."

At that point I found myself standing surprised, greeting her once more and ordered a seat for her and water to be given to her as she had arrived walking during a scorching noon heat. I immediately went to Garang to inform him about the arrival of his aunt from the direction of Ayod.

He looked surprised then responded coolly. I came to know that his aunt, Gak or Gangthi (literally small Gak or junior Gak), had been such a long time married and living in Ayod. Since that time Garang as well as most members of his extended family had lost contact with her.

We were told that since her marriage, she never went out of Ayod area even to Duk, which was near the home area of Aborom village in what is now Twic East County. Even Garang himself could not conceal his surprise to hear of her being in Ulang. Mixed with great excitement of a person who has received unexpected and good news, Garang could remember he had one of his aunts living somewhere around Ayod. But he had not seen her and had no chance to visit those areas since he began to run from city to city overseas, far from those places, pursuing his education since the time his uncle took him to school in Tonj, over forty years since the early 1950s.

Garang told me that at the time they were talking he still remembered his aunt's face despite the long separation between them. He told me, in a voice that sounded loaded with nostalgia, to let her in. Then he told us to leave them alone, which was done leaving Jumma and Obiech, two of his bodyguards. We complied and left, and soon after, we saw them embrace each other warmly.

She kissed him on the right side of his hairy cheek, while calling her long-departed sister, "Oh, Gak, Gak, I saw her," like people would plead to long gone ancestors.

I imagined her supplicating, expressing herself in lieu of the right word, one would call it "classical Nuer", with blessings to which Garang the "child" was humming his responses in his struggle to use the few words of Nuer language he could muster, while stooping.

We left the two that evening with a translator who took her later to where she was served and spent the night. Because of the operational mode we were in, Garang sent for me early in the morning, to let his aunt be taken to Ayod in the very truck, which was loading rations and ammunition for Cdr Salva Kiir. He asked me to arrange this since I was overseeing the logistics unit, besides the political work, as head of the political officer of the Bright Star Campaign. After securing her means of transport, I went ahead to supply her with some bags of maize, a bag of beans, a tin of edible oil, pieces of soap and salt, without informing Garang about the details. He had nothing to give to his aunt from the army stocks nor had he anything private in hand to offer his aunt.

The commander in chief had nothing to do with the distribution of rations, which belonged to the army. Those were issues left to juniors responsible for them. He just could not interfere in any assignment given to his juniors, unless there were reports about grave misuse or important assistance was needed for big groups of people or forces on the march that would entail his intervention. To interfere with what was assigned to junior ranks was to inject confusion and disrespect to the army of volunteers, which would disunite and scatter them, setting a bad precedent. Garang was with his aunt that morning at the time Cdr Salva Kiir was leaving us, and we all went out to see him off, including Garang. We saw them cross Sobat in a canoe to take the two trucks across the river and waved their greetings when the trucks started to move to Ayod. And that was how Garang saw off his only living aunt after more than forty years.

15

Priming for a Tough Mission

Right from the time Garang accepted to lead the movement, Dr Peter Nyot Kok put this question to me: "Do you think Garang will lead us to victory? Is he really prepared to lead?"

"I believe Garang is prepared. If he finds those who can assist him, we will make it," was my response.

Garang was prepared to establish a broad-based national democratic movement with a formidable force, the SPLA, to wage the war of liberation, to defend the movement and its members, comprised of all the marginalised people of Sudan, mostly from the outlying regions of the country. A strong force that transcends religion, race, gender, tribal and social differences. That move was informed by the history of our people in Southern Sudan, the Nuba Mountains, Blue Nile and Darfur, where heroic wars of resistance were being waged against the Turko–Egyptian occupation of 1812–1884, the Mahdiyya period of 1884–1898, the Condominium rule from 1898–1956 and the misrule by the Northern dominated system from 1956, that ended with the birth of the Republic of South Sudan on July 11, 2011.

Garang built his political discourse on the equality of the Sudanese people and demonstrated to all the marginalised to face any notion of subjugation. The first letters we received from him were directed to his colleagues from the former Anya Nya officers and people we knew. He asked us to send him people from the west, east, north and central parts of the Sudan without any distinction. We delivered the letters to some people personally and most of them responded positively. We in Khartoum had an organised clandestine office with branches and contacts all over the country.

One of the great successes of John Garang was the political and military might he pondered over and how to create it over the years. When that idea finally became a reality, it was able to coalesce all the oppressed nationalities and the patriotic members of the intelligentsia countrywide, controlled and mended every crack among them. But not many highly-educated people and professionals joined the field, which left an irreparable gap between the lower stratum of our people and the higher. There were a few daring youths from some African countries who expressed their readiness to participate in the war, since they witnessed *mujaheddin* flowing to Khartoum and into war. Some of them came to our neighbouring countries to express their solidarity with the African people. But they were discouraged until called to assist the movement and that door was left ajar for eventualities.

New batches of recruits were enrolled and given political orientation and military training, before being commissioned. Some joined specialised courses whenever there was a chance, which was rare. Every group was given a name and trained to appreciate all the challenges ahead and strengthen their resolve, which would link them to the struggling African liberation movements once organised and oriented to learn about revolutionary names internationally. I was trained and assigned to command Lumumba II, Neto II and William Deng Nhial II task forces, which were amalgamated into a brigade, based in Kapoeta in 1989 and later moved to liberate Kajo Keji, Kaya as well as an attack on Yei. The movement interacted with several revolutionaries and met them on different occasions around common issues of concern.

****

We who were members of the underground cell consisted of: Dr Lam Akol Ajawin, Dr Peter Nyot Kok, Daniel Deng Yong, Colonel Gordon Muortat, Colonel Edward Peter, Ambassador Manyang Awuol, Lieutenant Colonel Ramadhan Abugor, Dr Mom Mum Kou Nhial, Lieutenant Colonel Paterno Atari, Lieutenant Yohannes Yor Okiech, Daniel Kodi Angelo, Lieutenant Colonel Nikanora Magar Achiek and me. And most of us had specific assignments. After the birth of SPLM/A in July 1983 at Gore in Ethiopia and after the release declaration (public statement) of the manifesto, Lam Akol was assigned to chair our group in Khartoum assisted by myself. Lam took part in the drafting of the manifesto. John Garang never turned down what we recommended for being an important office, attached to the office of the Chairman, in which I was left in charge of communication.

One recommendation, which was adopted by the movement as a policy, was a request from the Sudanese people and all the forces of the *intifada* (Arabic for uprising) on April 8, 1985. There was a determination by the people never to retreat from the streets or hand over power to the Minister of Defence of Jaafar Mohammed Nimeiri, Field Marshal Abdel-Rahman Suwar Dahab, but to continue uprising until the army handed over power to people and returned to the barracks. That stand basically originated from our cell in Khartoum. It was unfortunate that the *intifada* was hijacked during the day and people began to wonder what was going to happen next. Dr Walter Kunijwok, Dr Lam Akol and Dr Peter Kok were instrumental in trying to convince the forces of the *intifada* to keep on in the streets until the army gave up.

But fortunately, that mob without leadership, were able to hold the Islamists from the waist, as they were attempting to infiltrate the Supreme Council of State. To give our suggestion a cover, we had to involve some personalities from the Sudan African Congress (SAC) in our SPLM activities. Afterwards we met Brigadier Osman Abdalla, the spokesperson of the Transitional Military Council, to inform them about our resolve to participate in the cabinet with four positions: services, economics, sovereignty, and an advisor to the Supreme Council of State. Right in the corridors of power, there were some senior Southern Sudanese army officers, who were summoned to meet Brigadier Osman Abdalla, a leading and loquacious member of the caretaker ruling Military Council that had ousted General Jaafar Mohammed Nimeiri in 1985. Awaiting ministerial positions, they did not know how long they should have the new positions and to where they would return after quitting the army, since officers leave the army after joining civil service and political positions.

In that foul air, we smelled a plot in the making, and that was where we knew the Transitional Military Council (TMC) would reject the proposal of the movement. But the final participatory suggestion of the movement came a day after the Islamists and pan-Arabists that dominated the TMC formed the government from behind the intifada forces, which they declared two days before what was fixed earlier. Dr Jazouli Dafallah, a physician and one of the leading Islamist cadres, became interim prime minister involving some selected senior Southern officers in politics without knowing the mission and the meaning of the *intifada*, to quicken their retirement from the army.

We came to know that the army had hidden Jazouli Dafallah in the Military Staff Club near the Khartoum Airport soon after he was liberated by mobs from Kobar Prison on April 6, the day of the *intifada*, and kept him isolated from the forces of the *intifada*. Besides Dr Lam Akol, Dr Peter Kok, Dr Kunijwok and myself, only a few clearly knew what was going on in Khartoum and we kept the movement informed about whatever development. Later the real position of the TMC emerged crystal clear, when Garang sent a letter to the interim prime minister Jazouli Dafallah, informing him about peace talks. Major Dr Riek Machar, as the SPLM/A leader's envoy, delivered that letter to the commander of Nasir garrison to forward it to the prime minister, which the Transitional Military Council (TMC) seditiously interfered with before it was delivered to the prime minister in Khartoum.

Those who hid Dafallah in the staff club were members of the National Islamic Front, NIF, and opportunistic senior officers in the Sudan Army under the command of General Taj Edin Abdalla Fadhul. This was coordinated by senior officers in the operations room at the military general headquarters of the pan-Arabist trends from a group allied to Brigadier Osman Abdalla and Brigadier Abdel Aziz Khalid. General Taj Edin Abdalla Fadhul, who was the deputy chief of staff for national intelligence, was an infiltrator and deputy to Marshall Abdel Rahman Suwar Dahab. They diverted the *intifada* and others painted with the Umma Party and in the colours of the Democratic Unionist Party (DUP). Besides Dafallah, a former pan-Islamist student leader and other activists operating in what could be branded as a political black market, they stirred up havoc at the University of (Khartoum) Staff Club. Public opinion was misled with disinformation about alleged links between the SPLM/A and the State of Israel—a lie fabricated to turn the Arab and Islamic circles against the movement—before April 6.

They began by confusing and frightening the president of the University of Khartoum Lecturers Union and the would-be leader of the forces of the *intifada*, Dr Seed Ahmed Hardolu. Then they planted an opportunistic Islamic activist, Omer Abdel 'Athi, in his place to present to the people a statement from *intifada* leadership in front of the High Court. For that matter, Abdel 'Athi became attorney general, who maintained the Islamic laws. Hardolu had to escape that same evening of April 5, 1985, to his Kamlin hometown, after conniving with the National Islamic Front (NIF), under the pretext of having a relative who was about to die. Although Garang was far away in the bush, what the movement he led stood for was acutely felt in Khartoum during those hectic days; he and the SPLM/A were stake holders that could no longer be ignored in the political landscape. Because of that, he was being kept informed of all the twists and turns of the evolving political developments in Khartoum.

Garang considered the problem in Sudan to be the case of a large segment of society being oppressed by a self-enriching member of the ruling class hailing from the riverine Northern Province, Khartoum and much of the former Blue Nile Province, who had been maintaining hegemony over most of the Sudanese people since the departure of colonial rule. The ruling clique, as Garang had branded them, adopted Islam and Arabism as their calling card, despite the paradox that their fellow co-religionists from the outlying regions such as the Darfuris, the inhabitants of Nuba Mountains and Ingessana Hills—in the Blue Nile region—have suffered neglect and exclusion despite their Islamic faith.

Throughout the struggle from 1983 to 2005, Garang never lost hope in his conviction and drive to bring radical change for the marginalised people of Sudan—the Beja and the Rashaida in the east; Manaseer together with the Nubians in the extreme north; the Nuba people in Kordofan in the western central region; the Southern Sudanese and the people of Darfur in the west of the country. The struggle was then to liberate the forgotten people of Sudan to enjoy their full rights as citizens as well as human beings. The first person Garang liberated was himself. He succeeded in moving himself from ignorance in its broader sense. Since his youth, especially during his student days, Garang visited Northern Sudan for the first time since the 1950s. As he was widening his horizon by means of reading widely on politics and in conversing with knowledgeable elders on world affairs of the time in general, and the situation in Sudan in particular, in addition to travelling widely within the country and later in the East African region, John Garang was able to liberate himself from mental poverty, and that in turn helped him to enrich his imagination and improved his performance.

As a person, Garang never put himself second to anyone but considered himself equal to any human being. Looking into the composition of our society, he called upon all the Sudanese people to stand together as equals before the law and to unite the citizens regardless of their ethnicity, place of birth or creed.

Garang made that crystal clear when he said, "Why should some people want the rest of our citizens to be Arabs? What is wrong with the fact that we are all Sudanese? That would not mean people should drop their Arab culture, which is also a Sudanese way of life. It has contributed to the Sudanese cultural identity. The same is the case with Islam, which has followers among Sudanese citizens. In this way, cultures, faith in any creed, language or race are attributes of Sudanese cultures and languages. Although these aspects of life differ from one another, it shouldn't mean we cannot live together in harmony with one another."

Garang put a condition for the Sudanese people to unite. First and foremost, the Sudanese should accept one another to be one to be able to unite as citizens and build the country together. He further argued that Arabism could not keep the country united. He went on to state that Islam could not bring our people together; in the same vein, he argued that "Africanism" as opposed to Arabism could not keep the citizens united either; nor could Christianity. However, Garang contended that "Sudanism" could unite the people.

Garang went on to say, "Why should I live in a country where I am considered to be a slave?"

The fact that he believed himself to be a free man was at the heart of his statement, which shook the very foundation on which religious and racial chauvinists were determined to build Sudan.

That point could be what Garang understood to be the concept that would underpin a realistic and rock-hard foundation for the unity of the people and of the country. Unless the Sudanese nurtured and endorsed the concept of unity in diversity in their vision to realise the new Sudan, the country would eventually break up because no other concept could hold it united by the will of its people. That was clearly the concept on which the movement endorsed the principle of the right of the people to self-determination. For the people to choose and determine, whether to stay as second- or third-class citizens in the land of their birth or not.

On that clear concept, Garang based the idea of the right of everyone to determine their destiny to unite or fragment a country such as Sudan, but that right could be exercised by peaceful means. In that democratic process the people of the region of Southern Sudan chose to opt out of the unviable union in which some of the citizens were less equal than others.

That was the context in which Garang sought to meet all the leaders of the Sudanese political parties, organisations and societies. He always met people on an equal basis, bearing the same national responsibilities bestowed upon them by destiny. With that broad understanding he extended his hand to all the opposition parties, which sought his assistance. Garang was out to help his colleagues whenever possible. He accepted to train revolutionaries from the Umma Party in Chukudum in Southern Sudan, in 1992. SPLA trained the Beja fighters who called themselves the Rashaida Lions of the East. He assisted the Manaseer in their legitimate struggle against the government in Khartoum, which refused to compensate the people for the loss of their ancestral homeland and subjected them to depend on meagre means of living, after having lost their historical areas and been forced to the desert to build the Kajbar Dam. Garang extended his concept of liberation, within the context of Sudan, to Darfur, militarily and politically because oppressed people, whether at home or in the wider world, should be comrades and must help one another in their quest for their legitimate rights.

Garang welcomed Abdel Aziz Khalid when he defected from the opposition organisation of the top brass officers in command before the coup led by Brigadier Omar Bashir, who became known as Legitimate Command. The body made up of the army command was overthrown by the officers headed by Brigadier Omar Bashir, a NIF member. He thought it better to keep him at bay, from resorting to the option of returning to the NIF in Khartoum, which might endanger the National Democratic Alliance and the government of Eritrea, being one of the leading factions of the NDA. The SPLA provided military support to other forces, such as allowing the forces of Umma Party under the NDA to enter Sudan through lines controlled by SPLA, which they tried to misuse. The SPLM did the best it could to brief its officers abroad to cooperate with the members of the NDA. Throughout the years we were in the NDA no criticism was ever recorded against the SPLM/A by any of its allies.

16

Garang and Politicians from the South

Throughout our history, most Southern Sudanese leaders did not meet as they did with Garang, individually or collectively. Southern leaders would accept to meet Garang but would not agree to meet alone as leaders under the same roof to identify their problems and seek solutions. If the Southern politicians had been interacting amicably throughout the years and had acted together, many things would have changed. They meet; roar and scatter, based on the way they failed to diagnose problems and differ without letting people know the essence of their differences. But resort to uncompromising positions based on what to gain from that sort of political game while stressing that "politics is a dirty game", forgetting that it is dirty people who turn politics into a dirty game.

But Garang always remained a simple, practical, outward looking thinker. He would see what was missing in an equation and what was required of him, when dealing with intricate problems. Garang cautiously based his response on honesty. The current world is full of complex problems. But there are multiple ways and means to handle problems considering the need for anyone to enrich their knowledge by learning from history. To devote oneself to learn and know how different thinkers and leaders pass through challenges and experiences and how they contribute to deal with similar problems, could be another path to acquire knowledge. In that manner, Garang kept people who reached him on trust in an amicable way. He simply contributed what was required of him.

The first devastating challenge, which was faced by our infant SPLM/A, was the Anya Nya II who almost blocked the movement in Ethiopia. After they started to attack the movement, Garang allowed the SPLA to confront them in self-defence along Sobat River, starting from the western hinterlands of Itang in Ethiopia, through the Nuer countryside to Bentiu area. Many innocent lives were lost during those four bloody years from 1983 to 1987. The dark aspect of those mass killings conducted by Anya Nya II, whose members were mostly armed tribal warriors, was that they collaborated with the Government of Sudan, which used them as tools in its counter-insurgency measures against innocent civilians as well as the SPLA forces before 2016.

When confrontation between the SPLA and Anya Nya II intensified, the line between the cause people were fighting for—namely to end the oppression from the Khartoum-based system of rule and mere banditry—became blur. Garang understood the role of Anya Nya II, as a counterinsurgency outfit that Khartoum was using not only against the SPLA, but also as a means to destabilise the population in the war zones, mostly in the Upper Nile region. They began to form forces that were hostile to the movement, funded by Khartoum. Garang extended an olive branch to them to counter all that Khartoum was aiming at, to delay the progress of the movement and block it in Ethiopia, if not along the borders. He dispatched a peace negotiating committee headed by Captain James Hoth Mai and First Lieutenant Deng Mior to Nasir area. Gordon Kong and Stephen Dual were the overall Anya Nya II field commanders.

It took Comrade James Hoth from July to August 1987 under

Garang's directives to find a passage to peace between the two sides. Garang met an Anya Nya II delegation in Zink near Gambela in August, led by Daniel Koat Matthews, the former governor of Upper Nile Region and paymaster of Anya Nya II, and David Bidiet, to conclude an agreement to live in peace and join hands and proceeded to liberate the people. That peace agreement was one of the great achievements reached to unite our fighting people and rapidly moved to overcome the enemy.

In April 2005 in Karen, Nairobi, Southern Sudanese groups who were associated to the National Congress Party, the (NCP) met John Garang after the conclusion of the Comprehensive Peace Agreement in Naivasha under the mediation of the Kenyan government of President Daniel arap Moi. Bona Malwal spoke on behalf of the groups who were hostile to John Garang, stressing the importance of including the rest of the other armed Southern groups in the administration of Southern Sudan soon to be formed. Bona Malwal expressed their fears that the SPLM in general, and Garang in particular, might not consider the inclusion of non-SPLM/A groupings in the transitional government.

Those hostile elements were desperately worried, hunting for a "space to be included for them in the Transitional Government of Southern Sudan". Garang replied by addressing them all by quoting Jesus: *In my father's house there are many rooms*, meaning that the SPLM had enough rooms to include them in the administration of the South. And thus, with only a sentence, that overloaded issue was resolved. The NCP was shamefully waiting to exploit that expected rejection of Garang, not to include them with "mouths wide open" to incite them by increasing their voices against the peace agreement.

Garang had many qualified associates, colleagues and intellectuals with whom he interacted and interchanged ideas in and outside the country. Compared to our few educated who opted to stick in the armpit of Khartoum over the years without making any headway to resolve the "Southern Problem", which they used to sing over the years. Today some of them insist on leaning on Khartoum to assist them to obtain more arms to fight the very people who were freed only some six to seven years ago. Garang studied and understood what he was aiming at, when he was the director of Sudanese army research unit and studied how to plan, control and use insurgents as a weapon and how to confront it. Intellectually, the real distance between Garang and many other Southern Sudanese politicians could be equal to the distance between Earth and the moon. It was not that easy to indicate where they could meet as far as application of tactics and strategies was concerned.

The way Garang interacted with people, his intellectual and ideological inclinations led his critics to brand him as a "dangerous communist". In their thinking, such labels would win them the support from the West, a desperate attempt that soon lost its steam. But Garang was eyeing some of the difficulties facing the movement at the time, to have them resolved when possible. Garang never cared about being branded as a communist or any other label intended to smear him and what he and the SPLM/A stood for. Garang was not a communist; his detractors used that accusation to win the support of the Western world and Christian leaders within Sudan, an important constituency that supported the movement without reservation. When we were in South Africa, Garang wondered, *If what one reads can help in finding a solution to one's problem, then why should they be complaining? People should not fear to know what they do not know.*

During our tripartite meetings with Anya Nya II and Union Sudan African Parties (USAP) in Addis Ababa, Uncle Joseph Oduho told the delegates, "No. We are not communists. I for one, have never read a book about capitalism as an ideology."

The hall went quiet, especially those (Anya Nya II and USAP) who might have been misled by the propaganda, and who believed it was their duty to redeem the SPLM from communism. It was common that many among political activists from the South and who held strong opinions on public affairs were loath to the acquisition of general knowledge through the medium of reading books, for example independent and reliable sources of media outlets. Instead, they relied unquestionably on government propaganda outlets: government-owned radio and television stations or partisan newspapers such as the *Intibaha*, the mouthpiece of the National Islamic Front (NIF), a publication notorious for its blatant lies and distortions. For his part, Garang always kept books even in the bush and acquired more during his often-brief sojourns in urban centres. His reading habits never negatively affected his primary goals of running a political and military organisation that was the SPLM/A.

****

Until 2005, there was no country on Earth known as South Sudan, the land where no single tarmac road was built. All the passages countrywide were closed because of war and intended neglect, which turned them into impassable ditches or streams. Over 95 per cent of the schools had been turned into barracks by the Sudanese government army. There were no functioning hospitals or health centres; most buildings had been ransacked and vandalised, while there was no single project operating. The state in which Juba as a city was such an eyesore to be an embarrassment to visitors, especially Sudanese who were visiting it for the first time.

During Garang's burial in Juba in August 2005, the Egyptian President Hosni Mubarak, who attended the occasion, was seated next to President Omar Bashir and the First Vice President, Salva Kiir. President Hosni Mubarak was shocked by the state of socio-economic backwardness and neglect he witnessed in Juba.

Instantly he turned to Bashir and asked him, "What is your problem? What is this?"

Virtually all job skills simply gone, and people became jobless because of war, as others ventured to escape. In Juba, all the roads were in a very bad shape and people led wretched lives. It was pathetic to live in Juba, a city of about half a million souls with numerous problems to contend with daily.

With that complicated condition after the sad loss of a charismatic, knowledgeable and sturdy leader of Garang's calibre, none could handle the steering wheel of such a country, to start building a nation. Lack of a responsible and dedicated leadership is the major factor responsible for the rampant spates of corruption today in South Sudan mounting to daylight robbery. Since nothing is based on the rule of law and respect for the role of civil service and its rules guiding public servants, the door has become wide open to briefcase business people, who care for their profits regardless of the means they use, including offers of bribes to those controlling the public purse.

Today, our country needs to be reset to follow Garang's blueprint. He would take and study a situation before responding. Garang was a thinker and one who did what he said and was always ready to reach the common people wherever they lived, as a dedicated freedom fighter. After the war of the liberation was over, Garang was all prepared to embark on the war to reduce if not eradicate poverty and social backwardness in the independent country. He was ready to learn from everyone including a child. He never belittled, shunned or shamed a teacher. And a teacher, according to Garang, was whoever had useful knowledge from which to learn. Public issues were public issues, according to him, which none should play with.

He once told me, "Look, people in the public offices always strive to have new things and discard whatever they have even if it were a useful thing. Better fix and use the old one at hand instead of looking for a new one, which might be unavailable or costly."

That thinking underscores what it means to be economical with scarce resources. A bird in hand is better than two in the bush, as the adage has it.

Throughout the years of his leadership Garang consciously believed he had the lives of comrades, families, citizens, foreigners, friends and foes in his hands to look after despite war. He always moved quickly but carefully, and therefore decided on major issues. As a person, he was a modest thinker with remarkable plans and alternative ways of executing them. To him, the source of the problem was not in the South, but rather the responsibility lay with the North that had an inherent and added fundamental problem with roots in history. Beginning with slave trade, the Northern Sudanese took an active part in capturing and selling the people from Southern Sudan, Nuba Mountains and Southern Blue Nile. As if that was not bad enough, the Northern ruling class embarked on the exclusion of citizens in those areas from taking part in the effective rule of the country. As well, the provision of social services and development of human and abundant natural resources found in the peripheral regions was not allowed.

The continuation of those deep-rooted contradictions in the history of Northern Sudan became the stumbling blocks to finding solutions to the problem of governance. Failure by the leaders of the North to find amicable and practical solutions had the potential to break up the current country and its fragile power structure.

With positive gestures, Garang believed himself to be a continuation of the leadership of the struggle of the oppressed people, which was continued by Lieutenant Ronaldo Loyola, one of the officers who masterminded the 1955 mutiny in Torit, where he gave himself up willingly and was executed, sentenced to death by General Ibrahim Abboud. That line of martyrdom included patriots such as General Paul Ali Gbuatala. William Deng Nhial, Henry Lul, Ngachigak Nyachiluk, Yousif Kuwa and many martyrs. Garang consciously took himself for a person chosen by destiny to continue the struggle. That cardinal fact moulded him to be an enduring, humble, responsible, valiant and a diligent struggler.

Tirelessly digging into the chronicles of time, one found no difference essentially between leaders like Ali Abdel Latif, Paul Ali Gbuatala, Buth Diu, Stanislaus Paysama Abdalla, Benjamin Lwoki, Bullen Alier, William Deng Nhial, Fr Saturnino Ohure, Ferdinand Adyang, Aggrey Jaden, Yousif Kuwa, Clement Mboro, Dr Mansour Khalid, Gordon Muortat, Luigi Adwok, Joseph Garang, Hilary Logali, Rev Philip Gaboush, Faustino Roro, Abel Alier, Ager Gum Akol, Daoud Bolaad, Samuel Abu John Kabashi, General Joseph Lagu to Dr John Garang. For instance, they all talked and agreed on the inappropriateness of applying the Sharia laws in a culturally, ethnically, socially and religiously diverse country, being a militating reality. They stressed the wisdom of uniting the country by devolving power to the regions through democratic and equitable ways. They also expressed their opinions about the importance of sharing wealth through equitable and just means. They sincerely stressed the importance of letting the Sudanese people free to develop in harmony, to live and express their cultures. But Garang had a different style and political direction, as a man leading a broad-based movement. Those leaders only recognised the importance of being a Sudanese more than being an Arab or African to build a home for all. But they never examined how to be a Sudanese based on "Sudanism", deeper than to be mere Sudanese.

Unfortunately, only a few intellectuals were awakened in the northern parts of the Sudan with courage to humbly follow distinguished intellectuals like Dr Mansour Khalid, Ustaz Farouq Abu Eissa, Ustaz Mahmoud Mohammed Taha, Dr Amin Mekki Medani, Anwar Al-Haj, Professor Gasim Badri, Abu Araki Bakheit, Dr Ali Askari, Prof Fazel Jamaa, Dr Abdel Rahman Zaki, Prof Osama Abdel Rahman Nur, Dr Wathiq Kameir, Dr Abdel Salam Akasha, Mohamed Osman Wardi, Dr Mohamed Yousif Mustafa, Dr Romani

Gergis, Kamal Jazouli, Sharhabiil Ahmed, Yasir Saeid Arman, Salwa Adam Bineya, Yasir Jaafar Sanhouri, Mamun Baghir Mousa, Intisar Jumma, Ramadhan Hassan Nimir, Omer Abdel Rahman Adam, Farouq Hassan Taha, Kamal Din Wasila, Dr Mohamed Jalal Hashim, Fatima Ahmed Ibrahim, Abdalla Ibrahim Abu Tarbush, Afaf Ata Manan Ali and Dr Mansour Ajab. Millions of people were there to prevent the country from disintegrating. But lack of strong political will and courage to oppose oppression the way Southern Sudanese did, was lacking and that was the difference.

Those people could be living examples of how humble Sudanese were, leading simple lives in and out the Sudan. Without knowing, the way they were living could set models as to how a true Sudanese should live. The truth is they contributed unknowingly to people who could differ with them, by offering living examples to better the living of all the Sudanese. They privately offered a very simple example of homogeneity that unites people, the way Garang would not have differed with them intellectually, in understanding and in believing what can unite people with different religions, colours, cultures and social status.

During the release of the prisoners of war (POWs) in Yei in the presence of the former head of SAF, the late General Fathi Ahmed Ali, Garang said, "A state is a human creation like a vehicle. A state is a creation of human beings. No state has a religion. I have never seen a state going to a mosque on a Friday. No state, too, goes to church on a Sunday. States do not go to Hajj or Omrah (Islamic religious duties believers are expected to perform in their lives if they have the means to do that). If we die and go to stand before God, we shall be questioned individually by God and no country will be there," Garang told the prisoners of war.

Garang concluded his statement by saying that former prisoners of war being released, were ordinary but powerful individuals who were ready to contribute to the good of the country, regardless of their ethnic, regional or religious affiliations. It was politics that divided the country, Garang concluded.

Garang acknowledged the unifying exemplary role being played by Dr Mansour Khalid Abdel Majid, who was an embodiment of moral courage, intellectual acumen and unity in diversity, and who defied prevailing perception and barriers that perpetuated divisions. Mansour Khalid embraced the SPLM vision and endured with it to the last days of his life.

Garang accorded Cdr Yousif Kuwa Mekki high regards, and for that reason, he honoured that colleague from the Nuba Mountains to chair the historic SPLM's Second Convention at Chukudum, Eastern Equatoria in 1994, to which some opposition groups from the North were invited. One of the least unexpected tests took place, worked out by agents pushed by the Islamic fundamentalists in Khartoum from the movement in a very sensitive time. Some contemptuous Southern elders plotted to divide the SPLM by splitting it to be exclusively left only for Southerners and expel the Nuba and other Sudanese from the movement. Particularly, those who sacrificed their lives in almost every battle within the SPLM all over the South. Most of the plotters by then were not even members of the movement, but self-appointed elements, who were smuggled in as leaders representing nobody but themselves, and who had been planted underground within the SPLM.

Some leaders clearly made a claim in the conference facing Cdr Yousif Kuwa Mekki and questioned him on why he should chair the convention, when he wasn't Southern Sudanese, but a Nubawi (citizen from the Nuba Mountains). Garang, in his capacity as chairman of the SPLM/A intervened at once, out of his revolutionary credentials to contain that dangerous plot, which could have exploded the convention. The individuals claiming to be elders, implying wise persons, were devoid of the attributes which that label is expected to confer on the bearer of such an overvalued epithet within the community of Southern Sudan. They had to leave the conference, satisfied for having planted the venom of ethnic division within the SPLM/A. It was not a mere issue of misunderstanding the position of Cdr Yousif Kuwa Mekki and the movement.

As a matter of fact, let it be stressed, most Northern Sudanese intellectuals were petrified by a group of Islamic fundamentalists, who had snatched power from them after midnight, with civilians dressed in khaki like militia and indeed, militia they were, like Dr Muthrif Siddiq and Dr Salah Edin Atabani. All the fears over the years were kept in the name of Arabism and Islamic culture. The fact that Sudanese intellectuals were resigned to leaving the fundamentalists to play with the destiny of the country, became very difficult for people in Northern Sudan to face. They needed to identify them as one people and agree to work together in a similar manner to how the Egyptian Muslims and non-Muslims (mainly the Copts) did to save their country despite those religious and cultural differences that divide people.

The impossibility of confronting the Islamists to the end did not take place in Sudan. That myth frightened most of our Southern Sudanese, the country of the domestic blacks (domestic servants), who joined their masters to fight fellow blacks everywhere, even in church, selling the cross to save the crescent. Every totalitarian government in Khartoum had used the denigrated and oppressed Sudanese and succumbed to their oppressors out of fear or money. They induced some Southern Sudanese with position and money. At other times, Southern Sudanese would refuse to accept Northerners to join the movement. Yousif Kuwa Mekki and Cdr Yasir Saed Arman, hailing from the North, were among the first to join the SPLM/A under the leadership of John Garang, a Southern Sudanese. That meant that the two revolutionaries and other fellow Northern Sudanese were under the leadership and direct command of Garang and contributed as much as their comrades from Southern Sudan.

Their role was in sharp contrast to some Southern Sudanese who chose to betray their people in exchange for money. The sacrifices of the past decades made by the Loyolas, the Gbuatalas and the Mohamed Nur Saads to challenge the unjust system of rule based in Khartoum should serve as a reminder that there are two choices to be made: either the cause of freedom and equality or the side of the oppressive system of rule.

However, it would be true to assert that most intellectuals from the riparian Northern Sudan have not yet accepted Southern Sudanese to lead the country. When Garang declined to take the leadership of the National Democratic Alliance (NDA) Asmara, May 1995, he expressed his position in a cool manner to that heated meeting.

He made the generous offer, saying, "Let Moulana Mohammed Osman Mirghani assume the leadership. I accept to be his second. I see the north is not ready yet, to accept the leadership of someone who was not from the North. Now let us keep the unity of our NDA intact. That is the most important thing to do now."

We who accompanied Garang our leader to that meeting from the SPLM clearly saw the point, which he made although we were heated with anger. Our point was simple: *When will the Northerners accept to be led by a person from other parts of the Sudan other than the North?*

Dr Peter Kok made our point clearly: why should Northerners refuse to be led by a Southerner? But Peter Nyot accepted what Garang had said. For Khartoum was following our meetings through secret agents and was about to celebrate, had our meetings failed over the issue of leadership. Our Eritrean comrades, and the world as well, exerted tremendous efforts and expressed their goodwill for the success of the meeting. Despite its success, the Northern Sudanese who were our allies had not grown to accept a non-Northern Sudanese leader. As a matter of fact, our Northern compatriots completely refused to accept what could have helped the Sudanese to keep the country united.

That was how, when and where the first nail was driven into the coffin of a united Sudan. The SPLM was not yet ready to accept the failure of the NDA. But that was a clear lesson for every Southern Sudanese to understand what the future meant. Thus, our struggle was to be much, much longer than people expected. To change that outrageous archaic mindset, we needed to fight much harder and longer and to continue the struggle with unfading hopefulness and an unflinching resolve to build a fruitful future for our people in a democratic atmosphere, until our people decided what they wished.

Garang believed our struggle, which demanded offering lives and properties, was not a mere game of power sharing. Nor was struggling something to be shared among friends or foes for the sake of sharing only. Our struggle was an unending responsibility, which entailed the objective weeding of the undergrowth and shrubs grown by domination and the replacement of the olden ways. Hence, corruption for instance, cannot befit a new era for which people sacrificed lives and properties. Something we know, which we pretend not to know.

When Garang stood and quoted the Bible to explain a fundamental point, he was simply meaning in his party, the SPLM, there are opportunities for people to benefit from without any segregation or fear, whatever a person's gender, creed, ethnicity and place of birth may be. We all like to be free from the bondage of subjugation and we love to live in peace to prosper with dignity in freedom. It seems there are deadly turns in the minds of some people, who have been misled by the propaganda from the ruling circles in Khartoum. That has always been the grave into which some people fall and perish.

17

The Pool of Ideas: Which Way, Sudan?

In 1984, the SPLA emerged in the field as a force to be reckoned with. President Jaafar Mohammed Nimeiri came to recognise the fact that the SPLA had become a threat to his government. Jaafar Nimeiri was known as a leftist who broke ties with the communists in Sudan and the progressive world from July 21, 1971, because of the coup against him, in which he was detained for two days. Sailing in his newfound orbit to the west, Nimeiri became one of the prodigal sons of the Arab world and the Horn of Africa with some presence in West Africa. Thus, his anti-leftist role in the region was assisted and strengthened. What SPLM/A was doing, was not yet clear and understood in many circles in the western world. Nimeiri began to open his arms to the Western world, especially America and Britain.

The West, by then, had decided not to stomach the struggle of the people of Southern Sudan and closed their eyes and ears, in helping the North's pursuit of their interests in Southern Sudan in the field of oil exploration and exploitation. Some leading magnates from Western countries began to appear to do big business and related politics in Sudan. That was the time when Chevron Corporation, a United States oil and gas concern, and Kenana Sugar Company, a British company, appeared in Sudan, as the most outstanding concerns on the new market. In 1984 Tiny Rowland, a British tycoon, was approached by President Jaafar Nimeiri to shuttle between him and the leader of the SPLM/A, Garang, less than six months after Rowland had been introduced to Garang.

Nimeiri wanted Rowland to mediate between the two of them, to stop the war, which had become a threat to his regime. Nimeiri asked Tiny Rowland to convey to John Garang his readiness to end the war. Garang took serious note of that message. When Rowland went, he came with a real message from Nimeiri suggesting that he would concede to Garang the position of First Vice President, President of a united Southern Sudan (the Southern Region had been divided into three regions, Bahr el Ghazal, Equatoria and Upper Nile regions respectively) and six senior ministerial posts in Khartoum. That was the first offer presented by the Sudan government. It was clear Nimeiri wanted to save his regime after his disastrous introduction of Sharia laws. Dr John (as he was known to family, friends and comrades) responded in a clear message through Rowland that with him were eleven thousand comrades. Six ministerial seats would not suffice. Rowland grasped what Garang meant by that talk and avoided travelling to Khartoum until Nimeiri was toppled.

That was an emphatic rejection to Jaafar Nimeiri, which Rowland could not convey to the SPLM/A leader. But Nimeiri did not understand the reason why the war was still going on and Rowland avoided visiting Khartoum to brief him. Southern Sudanese in particular, and marginalised peoples of the Sudan, were not vying for a few ministerial seats. It was a struggle for justice, equality, equity and freedom that would necessitate the overall restructuring of the country. Rowland was impressed with Garang and asked him openly for his personal account abroad.

Garang replied to him saying, "I have no account abroad or

anywhere else in the world. If you want to help me, then you buy military uniforms for the SPLA soldiers."

There and then, Rowland footed the bill to provide khaki material for making uniforms, which became known as the "SPLA Group".

In 1987 Garang received in Addis Ababa a delegation of the Union of Sudan African Parties (USAP). The meeting was arranged by the leadership of the Sudan Council of Churches (SCC) then based in Khartoum. The late Dr Jukuriya Wani, who was Garang's friend, was the brain behind the initiative.

Like a qualified teacher, Garang turned to tell me in a whisper-like voice, as we took to leave him, "If we take talks with them seriously, with time we will win them over and that will increase our strength. And why not? What we are doing in the bush drives all our aspirations and acts as a unifying factor for the people. Of course, you know them all. We need them. We need their support. You know people are always right to fear the side they do not know, simply because they do not know how the other side feels about them especially, when one side is armed. When you interact with them you need to be straightforward. Be truthful to them, because lies have short legs. Essentially, our struggle is one. The only difference between us could be that we carry arms while the people are unarmed. But despite that, we all aim for the same objective."

He then broadly smiled and stood to wish me luck. He gave me those valuable pieces of advice, as we were leaving him in his modest grass-thatched office, sometime in the early morning at about 03:30 am.

Our journey to Addis Ababa started soon after that marathon meeting with Garang. We all drove to Addis with Cdr William Nyuon Bany, Lual Diing, Alfred Lado Gore, Amon Wantok, the guards and me. We were with the Anya Nya II delegation. Cdr William Nyuon was the leader of our SPLM delegation with Uncle Joseph Oduho for his deputy. That was a pure political mission. I was charged to be the secretary to the tripartite talks. David Bidiet led the Anya Nya II delegation and Uncle Eliaba James Surur was the leader of USAP. After two days, Garang followed us to Addis Ababa. After four days of serious deliberations, we succeeded to bridge our differences and put solid foundation for cementing our relations in a very amicable way. Basically, among us, there were no ideological or philosophical differences, but there were some rooted misconceptions based on misinformation and fabrications, which we had to resolve, and we settled them amicably.

On the last day of our talks, we threw a memorable dinner to our colleagues from Khartoum and the Anya Nya II at Gihon Hotel, in which a chair in the middle of the High Table was left free deliberately by Garang for the President of USAP, Rev. Philip Abbas Gaboush, who was supposed to be our guest of honour. But he could not attend that special occasion because of Khartoum's refusal to grant him a visa to travel to Addis Ababa. His coming would have been symbolic that, the Nuba have at last joined their African brothers openly, before everybody and in Addis Ababa the seat of the Organisation of African Unity (OAU).

During our meetings in Addis Ababa, it was resolved the SPLM should introduce USAP to the Heads of States and the governments of Ethiopia, Uganda and Kenya, which was done accordingly. USAP and Anya Nya II were introduced. It was Garang in person who saw that they were introduced and stayed with us until all was done. We had warm relations in the Horn of Africa region, from which USAP benefited, as stated by Garang. But it was clear that their problem was pecuniary.

Cdr Deng Alor took leaders of USAP to President Museveni in Kampala. Cdr Lual Diing Wol, known as Baba Africa, and I, accompanied Garang on his first visit to Kenya on September 19, 1987, the day Cdr Kerubino Kuanyin was arrested in Addis Ababa. That was the first visit of Garang to Kenya since he became the leader of the SPLM/A during which we were received with red carpet. On the second day of our visit, President Daniel Arap Moi of Kenya hosted us for a day at the State House in Nakuru. With Moi were his Home Affairs Minister Justus Ole Tipis and Bethuel Kiplagat, the undersecretary at the Foreign Affairs Ministry. President Moi met with the USAP leader, Eliaba James Surur and Garang, in which they briefed the president thoroughly about what the Sudan was doing in Southern Sudan in particular.

During the luncheon which was thrown to our delegation by President Moi, Garang took the floor and thanked President Moi for his hospitality and added, "Mr President, if President Kaunda is the leader of the Southern African frontline states, you would be the leader of Northern frontline states. It is with this understanding we came here to brief you about what is going on in our country."

President Moi was deeply moved and felt inspired. From that day, August 21, 1987, he paid full attention to what was going on in Southern Sudan until the day the Comprehensive Peace Agreement (CPA) was signed in Nairobi in 2005. Moi later chaired the meetings between the SPLM and Southern political parties and militia groups at Karen, on the outskirts of the capital of Nairobi, to test the NCP's sincerity.

One major difference between Garang and other Southern politicians was that Garang comprehended the Islamic concepts on which Dr Hassan Turabi and Sadiq Mahdi were out to build their Islamic resurgence. He confronted them intellectually and militarily. Both men forcefully decided to build the Sudan, based on the concept of Islamic philosophy in accordance with the world view of Dr Hassan Turabi. The Islamists had planned to put an end to the existence of non-Muslims and non-Arabs in the country, in the process of Islamising the country by staging crusade jihad against non-Muslims or *kuffar*, Arabic for infidels, in which over two million innocent people were lost in inhumane battles, contrary to all human rights provisions.

Garang succeeded to confront the Islamists intellectually by exposing them like never before by a Southern politician, as heard in his profound address to the nation in August 1989, after the Islamists robbed power by night. Militarily, Garang confronted the Islamists that included taking the armed struggle northward. That strategy succeeded in awakening the Islamists to the creeping danger that was going to confront their regime. When Garang later declared, "Sudan will not be the same again," he had that factor in mind. Time has proved Garang in his prediction right. The huge crowd that received Garang on his arrival in Khartoum in 2005 had shaken Khartoum, the centre of the Arabism and Islamic fundamentalism, to the core.

At this juncture, one is bound to ask: How could Garang, the man whose critics frequently accused him of being a rigid dictator, be the leader who proved to have the right answer to the problem of exclusion and marginalisation of most of the Sudanese people?

It is worth noting that some leaders within USAP were even assisted with cash to transport their families out of Khartoum through Europe for them to join the movement as requested by some through the SPLM. But being the type of persons who were trained to hunt day and night for rotten things and cheap glittering objects in Khartoum, they had to quit USAP to join the Islamic fundamentalist regime led by the NIF, under the delusion that their double dealing would remain a secret known only to themselves.

****

These are the same individuals who are still playing the game of deception to this very day. There were occasions when embassies of Sudan in Addis Ababa and Nairobi, in a strange move, sent them some intelligence officers posing as diplomats to contact members of USAP, who gladly accepted the government's financial offers as an inducement. Garang was aware of that behaviour, but it didn't bother him since he was aware that patriotism basically involves sacrifice, a path that he knew was not attractive to some people, not only the Sudanese, but all over the world.

18

Anti-Garang Forces Determined to Destroy Him

Garang was negatively painted and fought against by prominent circles, especially in the west, as being a communist and a dictator, like the time they were involved in encouraging division, which took place unfortunately within the SPLM/A in August 1991. Indeed, it was a false drama, which was orchestrated by the splinter-gang who hoisted the slogan of democracy, transparency and the rule of law, which was planned by coup schemers and their sympathisers within and outside the movement, to follow the fall of the Mengistu Haile Mariam regime in Ethiopia. That gang met, conferred and agreed on the way to set that scenario to unfold, as a run-up to what was taking place in the Horn of Africa and in Ethiopia in particular.

But sometimes human memory could be short. Today, people rarely finger point at those who broke away (claiming to have democratic credentials) from the movement at that time. It was a game played by elements who masked their ambition for power as they claimed being paragons of democratic governance and respect for human rights. But within a short time, their conduct proved their hypocrisy as they launched their bid with horrible atrocities against innocent civilians and theft of their womenfolk and livestock. And soon they began to quarrel among themselves as to who should be the boss. It was all a charade of musical chairs.

After the fall of the Mengistu government, whose members gave full and unconditional support to the SPLM/A, Garang's rivals and power seekers seized it as an opportunity to remove him from the helm of the organisation. The putsch makers failed to understand the complexity of the regional and international affairs and how they often have bearings on local issues such as civil wars or local leaders involved in them.

A sizeable number within Southern Sudan's intelligentsia allowed themselves to be hoodwinked by the traditional understanding that political leadership was open to contest and that every Tom, Dick and Harry with no clear understanding or realistic agenda for solving the decades-long "the Problem of Southern Sudan" would ascend to the leadership of Southern Sudan's rebel movement. For such individuals, what mattered most to them was the seat rather than how to define and get to grip with the issues crying out for solution. In that respect, the problem was how to topple the leadership of the movement rather than finding a fair and lasting resolution to the Southern Problem and bring peace to Sudan. But conspirators failed to get the leader of their choice, and on that account, they began to quarrel among themselves to the point of returning to their previous position–the enemy camp. The crack within their ranks was no longer a secret; it became public knowledge that it was not how to end the war with justice, but rather who should lead the struggle regardless of the declared goal by the schemers.

The attitude within ruling circles in the western world of the time was the baseless fear that the SPLM/A was within the Horn of Africa's orbit, Ethiopia in particular, that was allied to the communist bloc. The same western forces refused to accept the movement's diagnosis of the national crisis in the country, not the tired and misleading "Southern Problem". It came as no surprise that the same western self-appointed "experts" saw John Garang for his unambiguous articulation of the problem and how to solve a correct and lasting solution to it, as the obstacle to be removed and replaced by elements pliable to the narrow version of the crisis that was staring Sudan in the face.

Those are moments when problems creep, seep and infiltrate from all directions, bringing loss of life and property and hence, credibility. Once a revolution loses credibility, it turns into gangsterism. Essentially, a revolution must be based on a clear vision and discipline to guide it, the way Garang put it in his graduation address to Shield Five in Bonga, 1988. Thus, to correctly evaluate a revolution, people must turn to examine the thinking and the direction of that specific move and how it relates to what people aspire to and not individuals. Hence, Garang knew well that the people aspiring for justice were on the verge of liberating themselves from subjugation. That was what he stood for until the time he departed.

The first important lesson, which we came to know from that painful split, was the fact, we all came to understand and know Khartoum of the NIF much better. Those who were wooed to join hands with Khartoum found not a single finger to hold and thus, they correctly decided to return to the people. The other lesson was that we willingly accepted to reconcile with dignity. The third lesson was that we witnessed our people being murdered, but failed to protect them, unfortunately.

In the process of unification by then, actors had the final word. The instrumental actors were Dr John Garang and Dr Riek Machar. Both leaders had resolved to allow our people to reconcile, unite and move forward to achieve their noble goals together. The previous divisions, mutual antagonisms and bloodshed had to be stopped and replaced by reconciliation and unity of purpose. However, to the surprise of a few, those positive steps were not welcomed by the adversaries of peace and unity with justice among us. They behaved as if nothing of great importance had happened in the process of our struggle. But despite that, John Garang and Riek Machar succeeded to reconcile, stopped the fratricidal conflict and marched forward together.

That split was destructive and had reversed all the political and military gains the movement had made since its inception in 1984. But it taught us a lot of useful lessons, which we should not forget. One of these was that nations are not created within days, nor can they be developed within hours. After we achieved independence, all the detractors, who were engaged in that game, knew not how revolutions were organised, but spilled the blood of the people by hunting those whom the movement fought for over two decades. Some seem to forget the difficult stages people went through. Indeed, wars are ugly, apathetic, avoidable, but containable. The most brutal wars were fought in the past and atrocities were committed by their actors as we know them from history and know there were bodies or activities on the scene to denounce the barbaric actors and their deeds. In recent times, the emergence of human rights monitors could be a welcomed development. What is objectionable about some human rights bodies is the selection of organisations or leaders and masterminds of certain actions or failure to observe the laws of war, that sometimes political ideologies come into play to prejudice the choice of the party to be held responsible for what the reporters consider to be a violation of human rights of the targeted group.

19

John Garang: A Portrait of an Astute Thinker

In his major speech when signing the Nairobi Declaration, launching the final phase of peace in the Sudan, with these words, John Garang made it crystal clear to all and sundry:

"What does peace mean to us in the SPLM? What does it mean to me personally not as a leader, but as a brother, an uncle, a father and a human being? There are many here and elsewhere, who think that peace is about job allocation; about appointment to positions of authority; lining one's pockets through misuse or misappropriation of public assets or by lording it over others.

"Those who think this way must be reading from a different script than mine. We have more supreme goals and loftier ideals and alternatives. My script reads that peace is what people believe it should hold for them. Peace to me and in the depth of my soul is a promise of better living conditions for young people, middle-aged and the aged, in fact everyone; to the individual; to the unemployed and the destitute; to the sick and the unlettered; all over Sudan. It is also a promise to the men and women of South Sudan, the Nuba Mountains, Southern Blue Nile, Abyei, Eastern Sudan and other marginalised areas of Sudan who have suffered all their lives in a dignified silence, the loss of their dear ones in the war of liberation or who felt and still feel a sense of helplessness, a promise that we shall never betray the cause for which those martyrs have made the ultimate sacrifice. And theirs is a cause for better living conditions for everyone. It is also a promise to martyrs and to those who lost their dear ones on the other side, a promise that just and durable peace shall heal all the wounds that we have inflicted on ourselves on both sides."

That was Garang's belief in the cause of his people he was championing. He did not fight the war to improve his living, but that of the people.

To Garang, peace was something great, definite and objective for the sake of improving the lives of the people and not for self-enrichment. So did Garang see a revolution as something definite, sure and certain. Liberation from what, not from whom, was his main objective, a guiding star. To liberate a people "from what", instead of "from whom" was not clear cut as some people are tempted to think. It was, as it is, a demanding cobweb of complexes, which entails and details tough options including the use of arms, as a means and not an objective, to achieve the goal. The objective being: to affect drastic change in the human mind and remove the bondage, which prevents people from seeing the objective realities of life with clarity.

The persuasive arguments, which Garang persistently used to win support locally and internationally and to raise funds, and later the peace talks throughout the years of his leadership, will be treasured by generations to come.

The problem of Sudan, and "Southern Problem", as is the case with the other marginalised regions of Sudan, has always been prominent in the centre of the Sudanese political dispensation. The people of Southern Sudan, however, would want to be seen as the only people struggling there, within the administrative boundaries determined by colonial authorities. Those ideas have their origins from the Juba Conference of 1947. Southern Sudanese would tend to disregard the fact that there were Northerners who joined them in their legitimate struggle against all forms of injustice, however few they were. Despite all that, they insisted on branding the demand to be "the problem of Sudan".

Garang reversed the concept on which the southern politicians anchored their arguments with regards to Southern Problem and put it straight. That semantic change was able to win for the people of Southern Sudan with some important allies from outside their own region. The problem, as he came to experience, was undeniably brooding in the riparian parts of Northern Sudan, which had dominated the country's public affairs while at the same time misleading Sudanese people and the rest of the world since the foreign rule ended in 1956.

Garang took the North to admit their mistakes. Most of the Southern politicians, who refused to know how to analyse the "Southern Problem" in line with Garang's conception, came to know later the way to analyse the problem. One reason why they refused to accept the way he used to analyse problems was simply because they were not scientific in their approach. They believed that would make them forget the way they understood the problem and distinctly kept it as the Southern Problem. To Garang, it was ridiculous for anyone to blame the oppressed people as the cause of the problem of rule. It was the oppressor who was the culprit, he said.

Garang could hardly differ with those who held other views, since the intention was to transform the Sudan to become an acceptable home for all or let each go the way they choose. And he illustrated that scientifically with charts. Garang looked for the most practical way to explain a concept and how to deal with it:

"If you want to cut a giant of a tree surrounded by a thorny grove and shrubs, one has at first to start clearing around that tree before reaching the tree you want."

What he meant was that one couldn't achieve one's objectives before reaching Khartoum, either by capturing it or compelling Khartoum to sit down with one and negotiate.

That was what he did. He later added to his literature the example of how the Eritreans liberated their country, by agreeing to join hands with the Ethiopian rebels in the field up to Addis Ababa to the time it was captured. Then Eritreans returned to liberate Asmara according to plan and entered their capital city peacefully, without firing a bullet. And that was how Garang saw the importance of having alliances bound by the same destiny. That was a beneficial fruitful alliance, which brought victory to both opposition forces from Ethiopia and Eritrea.

Garang's consistent call for the establishment of a New Sudan had two conditions attached to it. The first factor was primarily our inability to decisively defeat the NCP and its power base of Islamic fundamentalism, which attracted the world to understand and assess the depth and width of the problem, as the war continued. The second factor was the humanitarian support, which ignored the political aspects of the conflict. The humanitarian organisations built their presence within the theatre of the conflict to witness the process of the talks and came closer to guarantee the package would be agreed, which necessitated our taking the second option, when the NCP was pressured to accept during negotiations.

Garang succeeded to demonstrate to the world the difference between having a problem *per se* and how to articulate an intricate problem in an objective and consistent manner, contrary to traditional methods of how reactionary political parties used to take Sudan as a stepping stone through its proximity to the Middle East, Red Sea and the Horn of Africa. Second, through an alliance built on history, culture and proximity of Sudan to Egypt, since the days of the expansion of the Islamic empire to North Africa in the early seventh century CE and religious following to the Middle East, then came the rise of colonisation.

Garang succeeded to liberate the Southern Sudanese mentality from the bondage of "inferiority complex", which subjugated the people behind borders demarcated between the South and the North by the colonialists, enclosing people in the grass curtain that blocked the Southern Sudanese political mind in the bondage of bagging for rights.

Garang went on logically to emphasise the problem, saying: "Who would really be the problem, the one carrying a person on his back, or the one being carried?"

In those words, John Garang succeeded to articulate what was essentially a Sudanese problem in a manner no one had explained the case publicly before. Garang later made that statement about situations in the Nuba Mountains, Blue Nile and Darfur, where similar situations of neglect still existed at the time he was speaking. He applied the same analyses to Eastern Sudan and to Khartoum itself, which made him more Sudanese than those myopic Sudanese in Khartoum.

When Garang extended his hand to Omar Bashir in Kampala, Uganda in 2003 after those bloody years fighting one another, momentarily I was submerged deep in wonder, as were people who watched the two exchange hands in an acrobatic manner. People were shocked as they found themselves arrested in that suspense. That moment, the environment turned dark in our imagination, although the forum was taking place in the State House. President Yoweri Museveni, the host of that historical meeting, witnessed that occasion with open eyes and gazed like a person who did not believe what was happening right before him. But objectively, one felt, the war was over, since the two main adversaries were able to greet one another and sit down together to discuss the common problems: John Garang and Bashir on equal terms.

Garang refused to be seen or treated in the context of being an inferior Southern Sudanese or a second- or third-class citizen. He saw no difference between him and any other human being in the north or elsewhere. Though some politicians from Southern Sudan preferred to see him as a betrayer to the Northern ruling class, none from the South could surpass him whenever, wherever he stood to articulate, act or fight for Southern Sudanese with utmost sincerity and dignity. Being the person leading the armed struggle of the Sudanese people based in Southern Sudan, as the staunchest opponent to NIF/NCP, whatever colour they hide in, John Garang did not address the problem as the "Southern Problem" from the angle of intellectual bankruptcy.

John Garang stated that, "Just, how can I, an oppressed person be the problem? The problem is in the North, whose leaders have usurped everything in the country to oppress others."

He took the South for a direction within larger political context of Sudan, which has a distinct identity and therefore, equitable rights, short of putting it as if they were different people. He talked about the tremendous strength, which a diversified community like ours could have, one based on equality and justice.

After the fall of Torit to the SPLA on March 23, 1989, Garang raised the SPLM standard, now the national flag for the State of South Sudan. People were dancing with vigour. In the Lotuho tradition, men smeared their heads and faces with sorghum flour while stomping the ground rhythmically in an anticlockwise circle, and in harmony with the drumbeat and singing. Garang joined the excited dancers, and soon was lost within the jubilant sea of humanity so that we were almost unable to locate him. Having been adorned with the traditional gear and colours of the festivity Garang's face, neck and chest were ashen with sorghum flour.

When he stopped, he told me, "It is within the diverse reality of our people that traditional practices can be taken as a positive reality to enrich our cultures and embark on developing our languages and social norms, democratically."

Garang, for that matter, was not against culture and their way of life as such; he believed they were part of the people's heritage that we should preserve and hone to be consistent with the changing times. It was the Khartoum ruling circles, who wanted to do away with our culture to give way to Arab and Islamic ways as alternatives. He did not hesitate to defend the rights of the people including the South, if not first, as the most oppressed part of the country.

There were interrelated issues, which kept the war raging for thirty-eight years in Sudanese history. One of the reasons for the war was the insistence by the sectarian parties and the Islamic fundamentalists to rule the country according to the provisions of the Islamic Sharia laws, and the insistence of those ruling elites on the dominance of Arab culture, which some liberal Sudanese groups opposed in the North itself. Finally, the continuous exploitation of the marginalised people in Sudan and Southern Sudan in particular, based on long outdated racial concepts of oppression and domination.

President Omar Bashir came out openly to state, "If the South breaks away there shall be no room again to talk about religious- and ethnic-related problems in Sudan."

For his turn, Garang responded, "Let us drop these crazy ideas that we must all be Arabs. Even God will not accept this. In His infinite wisdom, it is this same God who made the Arabs; that made the Nuba; that made the Fur; that made the Dinka; that made the Nubians; that made the Beja; that made the Shilluks; that made all the five hundred different ethnic groups in Sudan. And who is this to amend God's creation? Who is this to make this amendment? The person who will make this amendment would be declared to be an apostate- someone working against God. If this case of mine is put before God, I will win this case. '*Wallah al-Azim*' [Arabic for 'I swear in the name of Allah the Almighty']."

That stand, which should have remade the Sudan for all the Sudanese people on an equal basis to live and prosper in peace, was what the Islamic fundamentalists and other Islamic sectarian parties failed to understand but mistook Garang's statement to be an encouragement to atheism.

Garang chose rectitude as a guide in both private and public life when making hard decisions or choices in complex situations. Indeed, he would have owned more material properties than his critics and detractors owned because he was aware that wealth and engagement in an armed and political struggle are two different callings that never coexist harmoniously.

In 1987 Garang ordered all SPLA commanders at the war fronts close to the Ethiopian border to collect hides for production of footwear for the SPLA soldiers. The SPLA units with bases near the Ethiopian border, unfortunately, began to transport necessities straight to the markets for personal use, started by those who were assigned to collect them for the common use. In that way, people realised that hides and goatskins were lucrative commodities from the hinterland, long regarded as places with nothing to offer by way of trade and commerce. Garang did not share such thinking because he was convinced that many parts of the country were rich in resources, but those in power neglected to develop the available abundant natural and human resources and their potentials. Such acts of deliberate neglect by the successive governments in Khartoum to develop the resource-rich regions were the product of the ideology that a class of people themselves who arrogate to themselves the belief that they are more deserving and entitled to monopolise both power and the country's resources.

That mindset by the Sudan ruling class to a certain extent helped in sowing division within Southern Sudanese polity, especially at the time when the SPLM/A and all its personnel had to leave Ethiopia as the government headed by Mengistu was falling to the advancing EPRDF rebels in 1991. Eventually they took advantage of the situation that should have demanded unity of ranks and purpose within the movement, not an opportunistic bid for power grabbing comrades in arms at the worst of times.

Imagine the funds Garang was able to amass during the long years of our struggle, for the man to die owning nothing personal other than his laptop, heaps of documents and his laudable legacy? Who had the keys to the funds and other resources from which he could have stolen what belonged to the people? Where did we send him to receive, on our behalf, huge amounts of money he supposedly embezzled?

We want Garang's detractors to tell us about the place where he is thought to have deposited the wealth the critics claim he had pilfered? Who in the world today is bothering us, the Government of Southern Sudan and the SPLM to repay what was borrowed by the SPLM/A or Garang in person? That was where misconceptions started to grow wild within the movement, turned into mismanagement and corruption when the unscrupulous operators got the chance to exploit their seniority in a lawless situation of war.

20

Humility and Altruism Defined Garang

John Garang was a man of ideas, who stood for the democratic transformation of the country.

In Naivasha he told me, "If Sudan cannot go democratic, then what did we do? The way I see them, those people will continue to do the same things to our people. And what will happen?"

His democratic ideals were covered by the fact that he was leading an armed movement that had a vast area under its administration, while at the same time he was undergoing a positive political and social transformation as a prelude to the emergence of a democratic society.

Every step taken to enforce discipline within the movement on an elite was considered by those individuals to mean dictatorship. Some of them were apprehended and held accountable for the mistakes they committed and came out disgruntled by the inhumane way they were treated. They would condone the shame and quit the movement and fly to where they felt safe and start to file protests and laud their voices that, they were undemocratically mistreated contrary to the law, where there was no adequate law to cite. The majority of those who left to resettle in diaspora foreign countries could be pardoned, considering how they quit the movement while claiming they were still to be part of it. When they found no other way other than to return to their people, that was the excuse they gave for leaving the movement.

The history of confrontation between North and South, which was dominated by armed resistance in a situation lacking popular organs such as popular syndicates, political parties, and trade unions and societies; was static, since there were no appropriate organs to offer the development that our people needed. Historically, political organs were lacking in Southern Sudan until Garang came to play his part in the struggle. Democratic organisations virtually discouraged and not permitted to freely operate under that armed oppression, to play their expected roles in the betterment of the life of the people to draw a democratic process. Conventional political bodies were allowed to operate in the South, run by self-seeking individuals who had nothing to offer to the masses.

Garang was committed to what he believed about democracy as the only safety valve, which the SPLM/A should avail to the common person emerging from an entrenched historic backwardness to safeguard their rights. But we have some people who take democracy as a mere slogan, sung but never to be put into practice. Garang was concerned with those who think that the SPLM should be involved with the running of everything including personal lives of its members. But his time was too short to establish a true democratic movement.

The fact that Garang is dead and resting silently in his mausoleum, should not let people stick their "hands on their heads" and start to wonder why things went differently in the ongoing suffocating season dominated by opportunists and swindlers.

Early 2003 Garang and I flew to Abuja, Nigeria, accompanying President Yoweri Museveni from Benghazi, Libya. Upon arrival we met Cdr Deng Alor and together we constituted a delegation of three. The Chairman had a mission of his own and Deng, too, had his mission, in which he involved Garang and me. Garang's mission was a response to the request made by President Obasanjo to come and reconcile John Garang with Bona Malwal Madut before him in Abuja on an unspecified date, but that meeting became the schedule. It later transpired that neither Garang nor Malwal knew the presence of the other in Abuja.

Despite the element of surprise surrounding the meeting, Deng Alor and I greeted Bona Malwal. Garang was already in his room. The process of reconciliation between the two men went on the next day. President Obasanjo lay prostrate on the floor before the two men, Garang and Malwal, an ancient Yoruba ritual. Garang and Bona Malwal rushed simultaneously to pick up the "fallen" [stage-managed act of falling] Nigerian leader and host from the floor, so to speak. Before President Obasanjo rose, he asked the two of them to skip over him to signal reconciliation between themselves. After they jumped over him, the three emerged from the President's office happy, holding hands.

Deng Alor had the mission of collecting support from some Nigerian notables who were friends not only to Garang but also to the movement. We met some of them in the State House and they followed us to our hotel. Early that evening they delivered their promise in a beautiful leather briefcase, which Deng Alor was fully aware of because that was part of his mission, for which he was waiting in Abuja for about one week. After our friends left without opening the briefcase and even before we had to open it, Deng Alor informed Garang.

"So, your friends have come at last?" Garang asked rather sarcastically. He took a seat and said, "Ok, let us see what our friends have brought."

I was wondering what sort of communication equipment it could be. I became inquisitive about what was in the bag and whether

Deng had opened it before. I thought they were to provide us with new sets of long-range communication equipment for trial. When Deng opened that bag, all those who were watching instinctively expressed pleasant surprise: the contents happened to be money: a million US dollars in cash!

Garang then instructed Deng Alor and me to take care of the money bag. It was a heavy responsibility, making it a scary, if not sleepless night, as we had to guard that huge amount of money in a foreign country (Nigeria) when we were not armed, all of us including Garang and Deng.

We left Abuja on that afternoon in a presidential jet provided by President Obasanjo to his friend "Dr John Garang" as he preferred to call him. Forty-five minutes after leaving Abuja in that executive jet, the plane ran out of oxygen. We returned to Abuja wearing masks and changed the plane. At the airport in Nairobi, I handed the briefcase to Captain Kuol Majak. In Nairobi, Garang told me to see him at his residence the following morning. When I met him, he asked me straight about the amount I needed for my department, which I told him. I found him distributing money, in the US dollars, to departments and units for specific requirements and functions put forward by their heads.

The funds were spent on airfreight, fuel, spare parts and lubricants for our forces in active areas, especially in operational zones. Many comrades fail to understand the meaning of feeding cars with fuel before fighters. That was when I came to assess how our success in the field was what encouraged our friends to donate funds, in addition to the right way we spent the modest contributions Garang used to receive from his friends. But among us, we the educated, some of us pushed hard by poverty in its broad sense, would think that once one receives donations, your donors would turn their backs and would not follow what was donated and how it was spent.

Donors could be strict with accountability of the type of assistance they gave to needy persons or the community. They followed whatever donations and how they were spent. Garang's management style provided by friends and supporters to the SPLM/A followed similar procedures. Funds received ought to be spent for the specific purpose for which they were donated. That was the way Garang was trained to handle whatever he received from donors. People accused him of being stingy, without knowing the ethics he followed. The challenge was that he was leading a poor movement of poor people where people depended on what was donated through him. But his adversaries believed none but them, as individuals, were more worthy to handle what was donated to support the movement. My colleagues in charge of finance in the movement failed to raise funds and develop regular resources to support the war effort until victory. Only some individuals exerted their best to support his efforts at critical times. It was not an easy responsibility to lead a movement for the common and down-trodden people.

So, Garang was compelled to go stingy to attend to the needs of a movement that was covering almost the size of three sovereign states with no regular income or donors on whom to depend. In a situation where people were deprived to go into business to generate the funds needed to support the struggle. The SPLM/A is one of the poorest movements, financially. That was the reason it took our people 22 years subsisting in the bush. The leaders of the movement found it difficult to generate appropriate ways to raise adequate funds with which to run the movement.

Given the incredible deprivation to which Southern Sudanese were subjected, there were more reasons for that failure, of which the leading factors were lack of financial resources, shortage of the capital with those who joined the movement and a shortage of professional business people to lead in that field. The ruling adversary class in Khartoum, and those who defected to the government for pecuniary assistance, did not know those facts.

21

The Man and His Style

John Garang consciously and consistently lived the life of a hermit. That was another reason that those who opposed him could not give him abusive and demeaning labels. Whenever he brought a new plan, which they had never thought of before, adversaries would take that as a mere lie and disappear once it was correctly executed. Those were the inherent attributes of a decent leader. They completely failed to trap him as a womaniser, a drunkard, a swindler or drug consumer. He quit smoking the moment he decided to join the movement. Garang focused on his duties and responsibilities as a political leader and the commander of an unpaid and disciplined army of volunteers, whom he never paid nor compensated for over 22 years of sacrifice. For our people believed, by following his principles, not kinship, he would lead them to victory.

But like a bunch of hired hands, opponents desperately tried, as they are now trying, to discredit the man by knocking their heads on Garang, that solid rock of our time. It is unfortunate that the few youths, who are being recruited against him years after his death, have failed to understand the reasons for their hatred. They are being taught to hate and kept ignorant of the realities Garang had to go through by sacrificing his life for his country and the younger generations. Before attacking him in his grave, let people know him. On the regional and international scene Garang soon gained a reputation for his resolve, diligence, hard work, and intelligence, attributes that soon earned him respect and admiration at home and beyond the national borders. That explains why it was easy for him to meet and exchange views with prominent personalities within Africa and virtually all over the world.

The personalities Garang rubbed shoulders with included prominent world leaders such as, Nelson Mandela, former US President Jimmy Carter, former Tanzanian President Mwalimu Julius Nyerere, Olusegun Obasanjo, US Secretary of State Madeleine Albright, Kenneth Kaunda of Zambia, Samora Michel of Mozambique, Ethiopian leaders Mengistu Haile Mariam, and Meles Zenawi, Egyptian President Hosni Mubarak, Ugandan President Yoweri Museveni, Cuban leader Fidel Castro, Muamar Gaddafi of Libya, Meles Zenawi of Ethiopia, Namibian freedom fighter and President Sam Nujoma, UN Secretary General Kofi Annan, Kenyan President Daniel arap Moi, Ethiopian Prime Minister Isaias Afwerki of Eretria, Kenyan President Mwai Kibaki, Mobutu Sese Seko, Laurent Kabila, Sam Nujoma, Micky Leyland, US Congressman Donald Payne Jr, Ibrahim Babangida, US Congressman Frank Wolf, Hilda Johnson, Rwandan President Paul Kagame, Ghanaian leader Jerry Rawlings, South African President Thabo Mbeki, French Foreign Minister Bernard Kouchner, Mary Robinson, Egyptian Foreign Minister Amr Moussa, Joseph Kabila, Susan Rice, British Minister for Overseas Baroness Cox, the distinguished Egyptian journalist Mohamed Hassanein Heikal of the influential Egyptian *Al-Ahram* newspaper, James Grant of the UNICEF, Raila Odinga, Andrew Natsios, Walter Rodney, Tiny Rowland, Angela Davies, Farouq Al Baz, Wangari Maathai, Virgin Group's Richard Branson, American diplomat Andrew Young, Angolan President Eduardo du Santos,

Hussein Habré, Idriss Deby, leaders of Chad respectively, US diplomat Susan Rice, Dennis Nguesso of Democratic Republic of Congo and a host of heads of state and government worldwide, academics, outstanding public intellectuals, academics, writers and others. He had a powerful chain of friends, among them: Dr Mansour Khalid, Dr Milad Hanna, internationally renowned Ghanaian academic Prof Kwesi Prah, Dan Eiffe, Dr Francis Deng, Egyptian businessman Nagib Sawiris, Roger Winter, Kenyan diplomat Bethuel Kiplagat, Brian DaSilva, Professor Gassim Badri, John Prendergast, Ted Denay and many others.

On his first visit to USA on May 28, 1989, accompanying Garang, were Mansour Khalid, Oyay, Atem Garang Dau and myself. We landed in Atlanta, Georgia. To respond to an invitation extended by the former American President Jimmy Carter to Garang, on a Sunday morning, we left Atlanta and headed to Plains, the hometown of President Carter, surrounded by peanut plantations. We were taken to the chapel to meet the President and join him in prayers and attend his Sunday school. All the eyes of the congregation were focused on us, newcomers. Former USA President Jimmy Carter introduced us when he began to read from the Bible. After prayers and Sunday sermon, we strolled to the Carters' residence, where we were invited to take some peanuts roasted by President Carter in person and spent the rest of the day there until five in the evening, after which we drove to visit Fort Benning, where Garang had done his military course.

Garang succeeded in creating a powerful lobby for the SPLM in Washington DC, starting with the late Rev Redhead, who served as a missionary in Maban area in Upper Nile, Southern Sudan. To keep the case vivid in the American mind since we lost our great African American friend, Congressman Micky Leland, in a plane crash on his way from Pinywudo to Addis Ababa. He was on an intensive working visit, which he started, to be joined by some members of the movement to change the way Americans look at our case, different from that of the State Department, which took for consideration whatever was going in Southern Sudan through Khartoum.

Congressman Leland told Garang, "We will help you with $40 million to face the humanitarian and educational programmes in your administered areas. And now we will see how you spend them. We will be there and see how you do it. I tell you. We will raise funds by involving internationally acclaimed basketballer and a fellow Southern Sudanese late Manute Bol and others known to him in fund raising tours." When they stood to pose for pictures on the steps of the Congress, with which Garang was acquainted since the days he was a student in Iowa, Leland added, "See, we should start raising funds by a prayer breakfast function, here in Washington to involve some of my friends in the Congress." Indeed, all Garang's friends in diverse ways helped the movement to achieve freedom with justice for his people.

When we flew to the USA, our delegation consisted of Garang, Mansour Khalid, Oyay Deng Ajak, Atem Garang Dau and me. We converged in Addis Ababa from different directions in Ethiopia, and Mansour Khalid came from Europe. None of us had enough clothes, except Mansour Khalid. Garang had two suits, with one of them showing a hole in it, caused by wear and tear. That was the second suit to the one he was wearing at the time. In Washington, with some money offered by Mansour Khalid, we told some of our young supporters about that embarrassing situation. In response, they rushed with Atem Garang Dau and bought him three suits from the market and avoided to buy the same types from Watergate Hotel, which has been made famous because of the scandal—Watergate—that involved the US President Richard Nixon and, which forced his resignation in 1973. At Watergate Hotel, Garang was accommodated in one of the most expensive suites.

Accompanying Garang to the Congress in June1989, our host

was the former Congressman Mickey Leland who later died in a plane crash in Ethiopia in 1989 while trying to visit the refugee camp in Western Ethiopia. Upon arrival he decided to take Garang to meet the Zambian President Kenneth Kaunda, who was the guest of honour at a luncheon thrown for him by the Speaker of the House of Representatives. When Garang was ushered into the Banquet Hall of the Congress, President Kaunda, who had an appointment with Garang, was promptly informed of the latter's presence in town, and he immediately arranged for a meeting. On arrival at the hall, Garang was received with a standing ovation, and a banquet was later held in his honour.

Although lacking the credentials of a head of state, Garang was ushered into the Congress Hall of the Black Caucus during lunchtime by Congressman Mickey Leland, where the lawmakers rose to receive him amidst ear-splitting applause.

After a brief introduction, the SPLM leader took the floor and told the Congress members, including over fifty other guests, "I spent more than ten years here in America. And if I live for a hundred years, I would have spent one-tenth of my life in the USA." Garang went on to say, "Being a black man, I was also concerned about the future of the blacks in America as well as in Sudan." That short comment moved the audience who rose to applaud Garang before he and his delegation left.

Garang studied in the US at the time when the civil rights movement led by the Afro-American leaders was at its height especially among the black college students. That was what he told the Black Caucus. Suddenly, the hall stood while lowering dishes, forks and spoons and went into an ovation. When he was leaving, many Congressmen touched hands with him, had photos and exchanged contacts through the American embassy in Addis Ababa and wished them the best of luck.

From New York we flew to London, in his first visit to the United

Kingdom since he became the leader of the SPLM/A. In London Dr John Garang was keen to cover four relevant areas of interest besides meeting friends and other public figures. His first visit was to meet the members of the Foreign Relations Committee in the House of Lords. He explicitly told the committee; he went there to present his views about what he believed could resolve the problem in the Sudan. He asked them to support him since the British were the ones who left his people in that apathetic situation from the days of colonisation.

Garang visited the Foreign Office in London, where he exchanged valuable ideas, which were important for receiving humanitarian interventions in areas affected by lack of medical services, education, water and famine, under the SPLM administration. He interacted with the NGOs who were interested to intervene in the SPLM/A liberated areas. At the African Centre, Garang had time with the Sudanese community, where he talked at length on three main topics. The contents of those discussions were later edited by Mansour Khalid, a senior member of the movement, and published in what became *John Garang Speaks* (volume two). Among the personalities he met were Tiny Rowland, Bona Malwal and some members from the British House of Lords.

In the House of Lords, Garang presented an elaborate speech on the SPLM's vision on the Sudan's conflict. He presented a chart in which he drew three circles, with two overlapping into the middle circle. He told the committee that the middle one represented the one united Sudan which we dream to achieve. The other two were either federal or confederal states within Sudan. But to achieve this, one of them shall need the Sudanese politicians to exert a lot of effort. Sudan shall never be graced with stability to develop, unless the political leaders take citizenship and the rule of law to be the basis of any fruitful talk that could lead the Sudanese people to respect peaceful coexistence of multiplicity of citizens from different ethnic and religious backgrounds, otherwise Sudan would be heading towards disintegration.

I was rather surprised when the SPLA's commander in chief assigned me the mission to Dungu in northern parts of Congo to release six of our relief workers then working with the World Vision, who were helping our people in Yambio. They had been arrested by the Congolese army in Dungu and taken to Isiro deep inside Congo, threatened to execute them and seized a four-wheel Land Cruiser, which they were driving for their own purposes, which were purely military. Garang briefed and dispatched me to the Congo. Without further delay I flew to Kinshasa and to Isiro via Kisangani. I stayed there for 45 days trying my best to release my countrymen. But all my efforts did not make headway. I saw the Congolese army from a short distance for the first time in my life and I was surprised by the way they behaved to people. Much of their behaviour was typically the same as that of Mobutu soldiers, if not worse. It was so difficult to find somebody to talk to, because people were frightened by the army, and one would be apprehended once seen talking to a foreigner as I was.

After 41 days in Isiro, I went on a hunger strike for three days, during which I refused to lift the strike, until all the six detainees were released and handed to me. They brought the Bishop of Isiro to persuade me to drop the strike, because "God forbid harming oneself", as he told me. I answered his Lordship the Bishop and continued my strike.

I answered the bishop, "Even our Lord Jesus had to offer his life to redeem us and, so why not strike to rescue my innocent friends from jail?"

After my fourth day surviving on water only, they released the detainees and handed them over to me. Garang continued to follow me through radio communication.

We and our comrades, who had been freed, drove for three days in a vehicle that belonged to the World Vision, and which had been vandalised by SAF, from Isiro to Yambio.

When I met Garang in Nairobi, he expressed happiness that we had returned "intact, and with my people", and added, "Those were the places we were in as refugees. While I was passing through the Congolese territory—without travel documents—I used to camouflage myself as a priest, wearing a collar, reading the Bible and preaching. We were in that part of the Congo with General Paul Ali Gbuatala, Samuel Abu John and Uncle Daniel Jumi, one of the revered elders among Southern Sudanese. Those were tough times. Now you know Congo. Congratulations," Garang concluded.

In 1990 around Lasu town, south of Yei on the border with Congo, Garang, received a message, that General Paul Ali Gbuatala was "alive in his hideout at a bushy location between Maridi and Angudri along Nile-Congo Water Divide." We in the movement believed that the revered soldier, General Paul Gbuatala had died a long time ago and that was the reason the movement named a battalion in his honour, for his role as one of the officers who masterminded the Torit mutiny of August 18, 1955. Lieutenant Ronaldo Loyola led the revolt. After the mutiny was crushed, he was apprehended and later executed in Torit in January 1956.

The movement dedicated a battalion in honour of General Gbuatala, as the most appropriate flowers to lay on the spot, wherever he was buried. Garang became excited by the news that the veteran freedom fighter was alive. He consequently ordered a contingent from the mobile headquarters to fetch Gbuatala. When Gbuatala arrived at Lasu, where Garang had a temporary base, he stood to attention to salute the veteran freedom fighter. Garang did that in recognition of Gbuatala's seniority during the Anya Nya war against the Sudan system of rule. Paul Gbuatala was also one of the few officers from the South during the 1955 Torit mutiny.

In the military tradition, holders of senior ranks do not fade or die as is the case with civil servants. To follow the example set by the commander in chief, the rest of the soldiers stood to attention.

Many of the SPLA soldiers who were looking on, were all astonished to witness their boss saluting an old man, who was a total stranger to them. What those SPLA fighters had known all along while under the command of John Garang, was that their boss had always been the recipient of a salute from anyone, occasion or platform they could recall, not the other way round. At that point Garang personally presented his guest to soldiers, which lifted their morale.

Garang had him for many days before he sent him to Nairobi for a medical checkup. He kept seeing the general every now and then, because he saw in him a "father, an uncle, a comrade, a general, a living history and an iconic figure". That was the first time for Gbuatala to accept an invitation since 1972, when he broke ranks with those of General Joseph Lagu and the group over the heated issue of accepting the Addis Ababa Accord and the subsequent formation of the Regional Government. He stood very firm against the 1972 Peace Agreement and refused to bless it, until he passed away when he was over 98 in 1997 in Maridi. Gbuatala took the Addis Ababa Agreement of 1972 for a form of surrender to the *Mundukuru* (a pejorative word in one of the languages in Equatoria that was commonly used to refer to Northern Sudanese of Arab origin.)

22

Among Neighbours

Garang's biggest diplomatic achievement in the region after the fall of Mengistu Haile Mariam was his success in normalising relations with the Ethiopian People's Revolutionary Democratic Front (EPRDF), government and people of Ethiopia. Many analysts had believed that SPLM/A would collapse after the fall of Mengistu from power in May 1991. The same analysts similarly thought that the loss of the Ethiopian support that the SPLM/A had enjoyed would translate to the weakening, if not loss of John Garang's leadership of the movement. Since such predictions failed to understand the strength and the perseverance of a people's movement and the logic behind the people's choice of armed struggle in the first place, the fact that the SPLM/A did not only survive but also regained momentum and became strong again surprised many, including foes and friends in equal measure.

Many observers failed to correctly read the depth of the relations between South Sudan and Ethiopia, demarcated by the longest western-eastern borders between the two: Ethiopia as a country and Southern Sudan as a sub-national entity, at the time in which the SPLM/A was controlling the region. Joined by the most secluded backward parts between Southern Sudan and Ethiopia, those parts could only be secured by friendly relations between the two neighbours, marked by the presence of several nationalities across their common borders. Southern Sudan, like Ethiopia, wanted secure and peaceful borders between the two countries.

Therefore, it did not take Garang more than one year to resume relations with the Government, people and the ruling party, the EPRDF in Ethiopia at the highest level. Strategically, the two countries are important to one another, and Garang knew what those entrenched relations meant to both peoples. His success was that he knew what internal conflict meant, as a man fighting for freedom. So, even if one took it from a chauvinistic-opportunistic point of view, it would be better for the SPLM/A to use whatever strength it had to finish the historical mission bestowed upon it by the people against Khartoum to liberate the Sudan, than support President Mengistu Haile Mariam at that time in history. Yes, Garang was fully aware, he had no strength to drag the SPLM/A into another internal conflict. The only way was to have secured friendly relations.

One afternoon on May 6, 1998, I received an urgent call from a friend following the bombardment of Mekelle by the Eritrean air force and before the news could break out, I was fortunate to get in touch with Garang by satellite phone and informed him that war had erupted between the friends and supporters of our cause, the Eritreans and the Ethiopians. Garang was stunned and was struggling to suppress tears. He promptly switched on the American television news, CNN. My contact in Mekelle was right and Garang rang me to acknowledge my call to inform him immediately. We were not staying together at the time, as we watched the wounded civilians being rushed to hospital. It was a very devastating and upsetting development.

Garang was deeply saddened by what had happened. A day later he flew to Eritrea through Djibouti, back to Nairobi and to Ethiopia.

During those rapid visits, he exerted tremendous efforts to find ways and means to stop the bloodshed and resolve the problem between our fraternal countries. But Garang was essentially a guerrilla, fighting for the rights of his people.

It was imperative and proper that he went personally as a sincere comrade to both parties during the first three days of belligerence to express his extreme concern and deepest distress, since the two countries and their leaders at the time were strategically vital to SPLM/A and understood where we stood during those difficult days. We had forces in both countries at that time. The SPLM/A focused on guarding their positions, if ever they happened to be attacked by the Sudanese army, which had assembled a massive force along the Eritrean and the Ethiopian borders.

Garang was careful to cultivate and maintain cordial ties with our neighbours. He keenly followed developments in those countries. He once sent me in the company of Omar Abdel Rahman, Louis Natale Fiji, Adam Bazzuga and Abu Ali to Gbadolite in northwestern Democratic Republic of Congo (DRC), to meet Pierre Bemba.

His message was that our people should start building viable trade relations with northern DRC and Central African Republic, since both people were neglected for too long and suggested, "Let us start free trade movements between our people who share blood ties."

Although he knew there were no roads linking Southern Sudan with northwestern parts of the Democratic Republic of Congo, he believed such contacts would pave the way for future cooperation between South Sudan and DRC. We were required to start building friendly relations with that part of the DRC to stop what the government of Sudan attempted to cultivate, to harm friendly relations between the SPLM and local authorities in that remote part of the DRC.

Garang intended to prevent that closed northwestern Congo from building relations with the Islamic Sudan of Omar Bashir, which was very interested in building strong relations with Congo through Central Africa Republic to get Congo involved in coffee trade, timber, exploitation of jewels and wildlife skins in which Pierre Bemba was interested. The Sudanese army had looted Gbadolite twice, the time they participated with Laurent Kabila in ousting President Mobutu Sese Seko. Since then, Khartoum had been hoping to find a route into Southern Sudan via Western Equatoria from behind the movement, but they failed. That timely message from Garang drove Pierre Bemba to reconsider his plans and handed to us a positive response, to Garang, which kept peace and tranquillity between the two.

Early 1994, the Islamic fundamentalist junta in the Sudan, led by Omar Bashir, patronised Dr Hassan Abdalla Turabi and succeeded to invade most parts of West Nile districts of Uganda. Jumma Oris, the former foreign minister of Idi Amin, led the Islamic invasion. They were only left to advance to Pakwach on River Nile, to blast a one-hundred-metre-long bridge and cutoff West Nile from the rest of Uganda, then return to declare an Islamic State in Arua, patronised by Hassan Abdalla Turabi. That move would have blocked the movement from the Ugandan borders. Luckily, Colonel Jet was flying from Arua to Gulu in that helicopter. He saw a long trail of vehicles full of people approaching Nebbi before they could turn east, towards Pakwach. That flight carrying a hero of Colonel Jet's stature, saved the situation and the Islamists were driven out of West Nile District into Sudan. On our side, Garang did his best to retake Kaya and Morobo, which had been taken from us at the inception of the invasion, late 1993.

Without exception, the friends of John Garang supported him with sincerity. He had close contacts with the Pan-Africanists from the African continent and the Caribbean region. Garang participated in the discussions about the need for Africanists all over the world to unite and work together for the realisations of their goals. When

I accompanied him to Benghazi, Libya, John Garang and I, in the company of President Museveni, the leading topic tabled for the three leaders to review, was the issue of the Pan-African Conference, which was resolved after a five-year-long break, and the position of SPLM in that symposium. The three instantly resolved that issue. Three of us were to form a steering committee to handle the issue of the conference urgently. The three of us were: the Ugandan Minister for Internal Affairs, General Kahinda Otafiire; the Libyan diplomat Ali Treki; and me. We were to prepare for the Pan-African Conference, according to the instructions of the three leaders. There and then it became clear to me how his friends liked to support him. He endeared his relations and he used to attend to them accordingly. John Garang clearly understood how to deal with people according to age, mental capacity and status.

During the meeting, Colonel Muamar Gaddafi raised a sensitive question to Garang, as to why he refused to sit and resolve the issue with President Omar Bashir, who was ready to meet him, given the new constitution of Sudan in which the issue of religion was resolved. Before Garang could answer, he asked Gaddafi whether he had time to read the constitution of Sudan because that was an important point to him. Gaddafi responded affirmative and ordered for his copy, to be brought.

Before the copy's arrival, Gaddafi again he asked Garang in the presence of President Museveni, "Dr Garang, why don't you simply declare yourself to be an Arab? That will help us to resolve the problem, you see."

Garang momentarily was silent and looked straight at Gaddafi while thinking about an appropriate response to that strange question. That question to Garang was so outlandish to the point the surprise expressed itself in his contorted face.

At that point, President Museveni intervened with, "No, brother. How can Dr John Garang declare himself to be an Arab? No. How about if I were to ask you to change the colour of your skin, would you accept that?"

Surprisingly, Gaddafi coolly answered Museveni politely. The acrimony ended there and then. For Garang, such provocative statements were not new to him; he usually dealt with them with answers that were based on reason devoid of emotions. As a result of that, the meeting changed gear when they brought that copy to Gaddafi. He opened it, then passed it to me to read and translate, as requested by Garang. Before we came to Benghazi, we prepared and brought our copy of the constitution of Sudan with us. But the two copies were different in their layout. Most important, the copy with Gaddafi was not signed by President Bashir, meaning that it was not an authentic copy. The copy for John Garang was passed by parliament and signed into law by the President of the Republic. Gaddafi began to feel perturbed when he noted the great difference between the two copies. Our copy was in Arabic and the one with Gaddafi was in English.

At that point Gaddafi, who was uncomfortable, snatched his copy and let it drop on the table, furious for that kind of deception by Khartoum and stated, "This, this is not even fit to be taught to primary school kids." After murmuring some harsh comments in Arabic, which President Museveni could not gather, Gaddafi dryly smiled while turning towards Garang, saying, "This is a joke. This is nonsense."

And that was it. The topic of meeting President Omar Bashir was not going to take place after all. We therefore had to leave Tripoli.

23

Economic Direction

Southern Sudan, now South Sudan, is among one of the most undeveloped areas in the world. Until 2005 there was no single tarmacked road known in an area of about 630,000 square kilometres. Until 2012; not a single five-storey building in any part of the region. Until 2007; no lifts. Until 2008; not a single cinema house operating; no regular transport system linking different towns; only two paved airports; no regular electricity supply all over the country; no sewerage facilities in the country; no national airline serving the region; and economically, not a single successful person running business in the subnational entity, until 2005.

Southern Sudan was so devastated beyond imagination. The citizens in the region were deprived of all their basic rights and were intentionally denied participating in the management of their own affairs. This was the land John Garang was preparing himself to lead and build almost from nothing.

Even before completing his doctorate in agricultural economics and before he assumed the leadership of the movement, Garang took time to internalise the economic reality of Sudan and Southern Sudan. In prioritising his vision, agriculture as a field of study ranked first as one of the necessary means required for lifting the people out of endemic poverty. To Garang, prioritising agriculture did not mean vital sectors such as provision of health care, education, roads and other means of communication were not equally important for modernisation and socio-economic progress of any society. To achieve those goals, he emphasised that hard work was key to success of a sound modern economy required for accelerated and sustainable social transformation.

While addressing a public gathering—on the issue of poverty and public wealth—at Isoke in Eastern Equatoria in 1986, he said, "Poor people have weak states. Rich people have powerful states."

Since then, he continued to stress the point of how international humanitarian assistance, which goes under the label of relief, could be harmful to development, arguing that such a system would encourage idleness and dependency on foreign handouts and harm our development. In a situation in which our people lack the prerequisites required for initiating socio-economic development, hard work would be crucial to start development. Garang warned people against false perception about what would happen at the end of the war of liberation. In that scenario, he cautioned the audience that for the citizens to expect that they would have all their needs provided by their government. To him that was not being realistic. *Where will that government find the funds for that, if the people are not productive?* he wondered.

When Garang stated that Southern Sudan has not witnessed any tarmacked road since creation, he sounded like a person who had lost hope. Torn between the bitter reality he was born into and the modernity he was dreaming to achieve, he learnt to sharpen his vision. Born in an unknown mosquito-infested village in the eastern parts of the Sudd region of Jonglei State along the Nile in the centre of Africa, Wanglei, Garang was indeed, a simple man gifted to climb to the peak of knowledge in one of the most advanced parts of the world, the USA. In 1989 in the Brooking Institution, Washington, he was asked about the economic policy of the movement.

He responded, "Ours is a subsistence economy and therefore, it cannot be compared to any given economy in the world," adding that it had been plundered by foreigners as well as by the nationals. "There are no investors, entrepreneurs or business people in Southern Sudan as you people would expect." He went on to say: "In such an apathetic situation nobody should expect us to give major projects such as digging of canals, building airports and road construction to the private sector, which does not exist. And no one expects to find the State involved in selling tomatoes along the streets." Garang spoke at length about the importance of prioritising our development in Southern Sudan, if we were to sustain progress, adding, "I believe a lot can be done in the field of agriculture." The most important thing about his economic vision was that he based his vision on the realities in Sudan, and Southern Sudan in particular.

His main economic concern was to develop Southern Sudan on an equitable basis to reach the standard of Northern Sudan or at best to overtake it. Since the country has oil as a major export, its earnings should be channelled to develop and expand agriculture that should be the backbone of the national economy for both domestic consumption and export. Garang always stressed the importance of using oil to boost agricultural potentials, from the rural areas to the urban centres, notorious as consumers and not producers. In his speeches to the masses as well as SPLA soldiers, Garang avoided jargon and complex concepts, and instead spoke of what was feasible and within the reach of his audience, which was nearly always made up of both SPLA soldiers and civilians in the areas administered by the SPLM. To cater for the interests of the rural masses who form the majority, it was time that towns must be taken to the villages, meaning that basic services such as health care, education, potable drinking water, electricity, all-weather roads, and so forth, which have always been concentrated in urban centres, should this time round, be taken to rural areas. He made it clear that to sustain the development people must build a viable economy in a land that has "never seen a tarmacked road since creation".

In 2004 in Naivasha, Aleu Ayieny Aleu and I drove to meet Garang to discuss an urgent matter that required his personal attention. His deputy, Cdr Salva Kiir had fallen unwell and needed attention, which was resolved there and then.

Then Aleu took that chance to tell Garang about our economic situation, when he told him, "We know our people are backward, especially in the field of business. Now what can we do? I am afraid, we are going to be ripped off by our neighbours," Aleu said.

Garang laughed, looked down and replied, "Well, we shall do our best to protect ourselves from that situation to happen."

We laughed while he took note of Aleu's apparently strange statement. That is the backward situation which Southern Sudan was in at the time, when it was certainly leading as one of the most backward parts of the world, where no single lift ever existed until 2008.

24

Tactician at Work

John Garang was a brave and considerate freedom fighter. He was brave to the point of driving people around into panic. He was considerate to the point of making those around him vanish in shame. He was a daring man, who would not hesitate to enter the bosom of an enemy while talking to make them understand war as evil. At Bou Bridge, halfway between Tombura and Wau, we had to practise the tactic of how to address the SAF, whose members were confined to their trenches at night with loudspeakers from more than three locations, to get our message across. We dug our trenches nearby and addressed the enemy for one hour and entertained them for half an hour with nostalgic amorous songs. The moment I stopped talking to them, they immediately began to fire at us intensely. But we dug trenches where we located ourselves strategically, talked and observed where they placed their artilleries while noting the burst of the fire set against us.

Early in the morning, our signal operators intercepted the army garrison reporting to Khartoum: *The dangerous tactic the rebels have begun, to address our forces at night with microphones, from a direction which we could not locate from surrounding bushes to entertain us with songs to which some of our soldiers have responded, following the way our forces were addressed by names and where they come from. Last night, three of our men defected and joined the rebels after hearing their names being called out.*

That same tactic was applied in Maridi, and the enemy was frightened. Microphones blaring at midnight, a distance from the enemy trenches, sent shockwaves to the enemy and they withdrew with their commander, Brigadier Henry Akoon, to Congo. Maridi was liberated under the command of Garang, deputised by our gallant Cdr John Kong Nyuon.

Jekou, which took the movement months to dislodge the enemy, occupied a very small area which was heavily defended by the government. The battle to capture Jekou from the government cost both the SPLA and the SAF (Sudan Armed Forces) an estimated amount of two million rounds of ammunition and shells. Many lives from the SPLA were lost, being the attacking side from a terrain stretching from southeast to west and lacking much in natural cover such as bush or hills, leaving the southern part of Jekou covered by Sobat River. But it was important to liberate the strategically important outpost the government was using as a listening post from where its agents among the locals were gathering information from the nearby Itang refugee camp and the neighbouring SPLA training camps at Bonga and Bilpam (also the SPLA headquarters). Firstly, it was a significant border trading post between Sudan and Ethiopia, secondly, this demonstrated the determination of the SPLM/A to liberate every inch of all the areas under Khartoum occupation, and finally, we needed to convince our Ethiopian friends about our ability to fight and beat the enemy. It is important to note that all the battles fought had their own strategical values although the cost in lives lost was high.

In the battle of Jekou, for instance, Garang was personally involved in directing the combat. On one engagement with the enemy, he was missed narrowly when a bullet hit a nearby tree, which he was using as cover. The whizzing bullet flew a few inches distant from his heart. From that day onwards, all the bodyguards were alerted about safety, to pull out commanders even by force at times, if they ever insisted on not withdrawing when facing imminent danger. We sadly lost the gallant Cdr Francis Ngor Machiech near Jekou, when he refused to withdraw before a massive Anya Nya attack after the forces under his command had run out of ammunition. He was speared to death as he was facing his killers while standing with twelve officers who refused to abandon him to die alone, in the words of a comrade who witnessed his lifeless body on the ground after the enemy had withdrawn from the battlefield.

Garang would never rebuke an officer publicly or shun a person, however junior. He would call him aside and talk, although he would not hesitate to call a spade a spade. With his carefulness, he never surrendered to the challenges of life. He respected himself before his forces could respect him. That was why, to achieve peace and freedom for the people, he was always ready "to meet the devil without indulging himself or falling into sin".

One of the biggest delegations ever sent by Khartoum to the movement in the first week of August 1989, a month after the coup, was a delegation sent by the NIF-led government of Omar Bashir. Their mission was to approach the movement to "reach peace with them like soldiers" to deceive the Sudanese people about their seriousness to "reach peace as soldiers". The delegation was composed of Colonel Mohammed Amin Khalifa, the leader of the delegation; Dr Ali Haj Mohammed; Lieutenant General Yousif Ahmed Yusif; Dr Fadl Saed Abu Geseisa; Brigadier Kamal Ali Mukhtar; Brig Ahmed Nassar; Brigadier Mathiang Malual; Musa Said Ahmed and Musa Ali Bilal. That delegation was so excited to be in Addis Ababa, before meeting Mengistu Haile Mariam.

After spending four days in Addis Ababa, they finally met President

Mengistu Haile Mariam, who gave them one of the toughest lessons, which they could not forget.

He explicitly told them: "Why do you come to us now with a plan to resolve the Southern problem from behind us?" Then he told them, "If you genuinely want peace then you should have come through our Ministry of Foreign Affairs and Ministry of Interior to put us in picture." President Mengistu Haile Mariam lectured to them heatedly for almost three hours, and he concluded his talk and asked the delegation to leave Ethiopia. That was how the delegation ended its visit to Ethiopia.

As they were leaving, President Mengistu Haile Mariam ushered to Brigadier Mathiang Malual from among them, the only person from the South in the delegation, to remain behind. He thanked him for what he was doing for his people and the movement from reports he received from his people in Khartoum stating: "That is how one should help his people." He then let him go. The moment he joined his delegation, they pestered him with questions about his meeting with Colonel Mengistu Haile Mariam. For his answer, Mathiang fabricated a story about that encounter with the Ethiopian leader, who he alleged to have condemned him as a "useless traitor working against his people". Upon hearing that, they all laughed and congratulated him for his "boldness" standing up to Mengistu, who was known as one who never brooked dissent. Later that evening, some of our comrades met Mathiang Malual and gave them an inside story about the Ethiopian regime and what it was doing for the cause of our liberation.

Peace talks between the movement and the NIF in August 2003 almost came to a halt. Khartoum had decided to withdraw from the talks and Vice President Ali Osman Mohammed Taha was recalled to Khartoum when talks became tough. Garang thought of a way to push them to Naivasha to continue the talks. He quietly went to Asmara to meet his forces with a plan to bring Ali Osman to

Naivasha. And he got what he wanted. He quickly organised a second limited attack on Kassala airport in the evening, which blew up two helicopters, incapacitated three tanks, destroyed a cargo plane and set fuel tanks on fire. That sudden attack on Kassala reminded Khartoum of the first New Sudan Brigade's onslaught in which the government lost Kassala for three days, and which caused panic in Khartoum. As a result of that, Vice President Ali Osman had to rush to Naivasha to continue talks with the SPLM.

Garang fully understood the situation when he signed the CPA with the National Congress Party, which he used to refer to as National Islamic Front (NIF), their original name. He agreed to conclude peace with them. But knowing where their weaknesses lay, he was equally serious not to let them change a dot in what they agreed to endorse in Naivasha and Nairobi before the world. In his last speech in Rumbek coming from Khartoum, he spoke to the people in a rally a day before his "final departure" to New Site from where he proceeded to Uganda. He stated that, he was to be deputised by Cdr Salva Kiir. in the South with full powers because he "would have to be in Khartoum most of the time to attend to important things in the centre." He had no other way to tell the people more than that. It was that clear, simple and straightforward.

Soon after he was sworn in at Khartoum as the First Vice President of the Republic, John Garang embarked on some of his undisclosed programs and plans, which only a very few comrades came to know. This included the dispatching of Abdel Aziz Adam Hilu and Omer Abdel Rahman Adam, known by his nickname of Omer Fur, to Fasher before he flew to Rumbek. When he went to Rumbek from where he had visited Uganda via New Site, he had planned to pay a visit to Darfur via Bentiu, on his return.

Before Garang could leave Khartoum for Rumbek, he arranged a special plane to be made available for two volunteers, who left for El Fasher in Darfur to prepare for his visit with Mohamed Osman

Yousif Kibir, the governor of Northern Darfur. He wanted to resolve the Darfur crisis. His plan was to bring together all the opposition groups to one side to conclude a peaceful deal with the government in the like of the CPA, while the world was there waiting. Garang was expected to sign a declaration to that effect at Jebel Mara and visit the three states of Darfur. But, alas, Cdr Abdel Aziz Adam Hilu and Omer Fur got the news of what transpired to the helicopter and to John Garang and returned in tears from El Fasher to Khartoum.

In his few days in Khartoum, First Vice President John Garang was ready to confront President Omar Bashir about the way he would choose to implement the CPA. When the Abyei Border Commission (ABC) team had finalised its work and presented their report to President Bashir and First Vice President Garang, President Omar Bashir objected to that, saying, "This will take us back into war again."

For his part, Garang promptly responded, "No, no. That [return to war] will not happen since both of us are here."

That was what happened during the first three weeks Garang was in office in Khartoum as the First Vice President of Sudan. At this juncture, he correctly anticipated more confrontations to recur, if he did not keep his eyes wide open within the Republican Palace. Although no military confrontation occurred under First Vice President Salva Kiir, similar disagreements with President Omar Bashir characterised the interim period.

Adversaries are usually at each other's throat. But people normally come to terms with their adversaries. Garang clearly saw that, as one of the fundamental duties of a responsible leader, to put his foot wherever his people have an interest.

"I am ready to follow the enemy wherever they go. And if I find them talking to *khawaja* (Arabic word for a white person, mainly of European descent) about us that we are not going to allow them rest, but to evict them out of our land, give me some guns to stop them. I will quietly wait in a corner until they finish, then enter to meet the same *khawaja* and tell him: the person who was here has lied to you. He is a real imposter. I am the real owner of the land and ready to share with you what belongs to us. Please, better give me the same guns and you will see."

"Peace agreements come because of adversaries coming to terms with each other. Peace comes when two or more parties in a conflict sit and talk," was how Garang put it.

Peace comes between those who have and those who have not. Peace must be between those who usurp the rights of others and those who stand for their rights. Garang saw it as a duty to confront those who misbehave, misread, mistreat and mistrust other people. The fact that Garang stood against the betrayal of his people, earned him many enemies and ultimately cost him his life.

Throughout my stay with Garang, I do not recall an occasion when he asked those around him for something to eat or when enquiries such as, *Where is my breakfast? What has happened to my lunch? Where is my food?* were ever made. Neither have I ever heard from anyone within Garang's permanent entourage that Garang showed or expressed concerns over matters that were particularly personal in nature. I clearly remember the time when Garang left us at Pagak for Zink, a small station near Gambela, Ethiopia, for a couple of days to attend to some urgent issues. On that trip he was joined by Cdr Gier Chuang. The following evening Gier arrived to find Kuol, Garang's personal chef was not there. Being one of the senior officers attached to the commander in chief's headquarters, Gier wanted to know from the guards whether the boss had had a bite. Surprisingly, Gier was told Garang had taken nothing since his arrival from Pagak a day earlier.

Cdr Gier Chuang was upset when he knew that Garang had not been served with food, but only tea and juice for about thirty-six hours. At that moment, Kuol, Garang's cook, arrived. He had been in

Itang refugee camp for the preceding four days. Gier was so enraged by Kuol's conduct that he had to be restrained by other guards when he was about to physically attack him. After cooling down, Gier there and then ordered Kuol's immediate transfer from the commander in chief's headquarters. All that was taking place without Garang's knowledge since the row was out of his earshot. There was a high probability that he would have intervened to stop both the row and transfer, all were a reaction to his personal welfare that Gier judged was neglected by Kuol. Throughout the time I was with Garang, it was common knowledge that he never asked for food wherever he was, either at home, in the field or during his foreign tours. I never heard him do so all the time I was in the headquarters, not far from him.

While in the Libyan capital, when word came that he was to meet Colonel Gaddafi at Sirte, Garang had a very short time to prepare for the meeting. He had to rush straight to the airport in his casual dress. Without prior arrangement and in a typical guerrilla style of constantly sharing whatever we had, since Garang and I were of similar size and height, I removed my jacket and passed it to him as we were rushing to the plane. (Deng Alor was far taller and slenderer than Garang.) To our relief, Garang took the jacket, put it on and boarded the plane. At that specific moment, I watched Garang boarding the plane and saw his humility as he was being accompanied by his wife, Rebecca Nyandeng, Deng Alor, Omer Abdel Rahman, known by his nickname as Fur, Susan Jambo and Kuol Majak.

In fact, we were all sweating profusely, and mad with anger, when we learnt our Libyan friends had clandestinely planned a meeting between Omar Bashir and Garang to take place within the corridors of the Organisation of African Unity (OAU) summit at Sirte 1999, a day before its name changed to African Union (AU). The meeting failed to take place as the Libyans and their Sudanese counterparts had wished, because of our collective objection to the odious trap.

We all had to hold hands together symbolically, to repulse whoever would attempt to ask for Garang. They left and after two days Garang returned me the jacket in Tripoli with a note of thanks and appreciation when he departed Sirte for home through Abuja. Who today can do such a thing? The man—Colonel Muamar Qaddafi—did what we told him: not to meet Omar Bashir. He complied.

Many people knew not when Garang went to bed. In the field, he was always up throughout the night working, reading or watching a film of interest. In the headquarters, guards attended to him in turns throughout the night. He slept a little but read almost all the time during his flights. At times we would intervene, when there was a chain of people waiting for him. Garang spent most of his time either meeting, writing, reading, strategising, listening to radio, watching news and current affairs on TV, videos, Internet or on telephones and radio stations. We stood for a long time during operations where he used to spend his time following the events from his command post, while doing things like roasting meat, fish or fixing food for his forces who were engaged in the battlefield.

Around Juba in 1992, when we were attacking, he beckoned me to accompany him to where food was being prepared for those who were returning from the battle. I understood that we were going to cook for our forces. He looked happy to do that without being chauvinistic. He would remember his school days when he used to cook.

"Oh, yes, I used to like preparing fish. By the way, when we were students at Tonj [Intermediate School in the late 1950s], I was one of the best cooks in our group. To this day, fried fish is one of my favourites."

We participated on an equal basis with other cooks to prepare the meal. I was with the team preparing beans and he joined the team dishing the food. Our fighters were surprised when they discovered that it was Garang himself who was serving them food with some jokes to top his service. That made our fighters so happy.

In Naivasha he took to sports quite readily. It seemed he was preparing himself to be fit for his expected responsibilities. He was up early each morning to prepare himself for his appointments, whenever, wherever the meetings were. He liked to watch hippopotamus grazing under his balcony in the evening in the Simba Lodge in Naivasha. When I visited him on the veranda of his room, he told me he enjoyed watching the natural world of the wildlife nearby and that gave his mind a break from the peace talks that consumed much of his waking time. He also loved watching people performing traditional dance whenever he had time to spare during his lightning visit to the countryside of areas under the SPLM/A administration. Wherever he was, Garang usually slept for less than five hours a day.

But above all, Garang had to respond to all urgent massages, which kept flowing in from the field and from nearly all corners of the earth, a situation that forced him to prioritise his response to them. At the same time, he was able to receive almost every individual, mostly foreign VIPs [very important persons] or their representatives, who wanted to meet him wherever he was. Although such meetings used to consume his valuable time, he once admitted that such contacts and meetings constituted an invaluable source of information in diverse fields. "People [he met] keep me informed." In other words, Garang was one of the most informed political leaders about either local, regional or international affairs of his day. He effectively utilised such knowledge in the interests of the armed political and military struggle he was spearheading.

Theoretical knowledge to Garang was not enough. Whenever, he had time to spare he would travel to some rural areas under the administration of the SPLM/A to meet the inhabitants and their leaders on the spot. After the liberation of a large swathe of land in Bahr el Ghazal in 2003, he travelled extensively there. That tour began in Thiet in Tonj area and covered many other areas east and west of Jur

River to the village where his first deputy, Cdr Salva Kiir was born, not far from Akon. For Garang, action spoke louder than words.

One of his neighbours in Haj Yousif in Khartoum North, where he was renting a house in 1983, was an ordinary Northern Sudanese. When that man, who was a butcher, was interviewed by one of Khartoum newspapers about Garang after his death he had this to say, "Garang was my neighbour and a regular customer too. But he was a very considerate man. He never entered to his home without asking about me almost every day. As a neighbour, he always enquired about me even if he came late at night."

25

Commander in Chief in Action

Garang was a very secretive man. He always kept whatever he heard to himself, and used it if it had something to do with humour. I never heard him being quoted by any officer for whatever he said in confidence. He was not a sham commander who turned his back at battles. Garang was engaged in many battles and won, as a matter of history, except for the one in Juba starting from June 1982. That specific attack on Juba was waged essentially to save the movement from falling into the hands of two allied attacks, the Sudan Army and SPLM-Nasir faction. That attack on Juba, succeeded to hold both "Khartoum and Nasir" [a reference to SAF and forces of Nasir faction headed by Cdr Riek Machar] from attacking other SPLA positions in the South for over a year.

Garang was a prodigious tactician and a leading agitator who raised the morale of the rank and file of his forces and made them almost fly into fire, whenever launching an attack on the enemy. After the liberation of Torit, in March 1989, Garang was accorded a popular reception at Magwe, a county within Torit. He addressed the jubilant crowd that had assembled to accord him a hero welcome.

In that speech Garang said, "Did you not see them rushing in disarray to Uganda through this way? Did you not see what our 'Hunger Battalion' and 'Mosquito Battalion' did to them? Sure, you know what they did. You saw how weak they were. They are finished, I tell you." The crowd burst into a thunderous laughter and applause.

When he decided to attack Kassala on about October 30, 2000, his aim was to deflect SAF operations against the SPLA in the South, the Nuba Mountains and Blue Nile where our forces were deployed. Garang wanted to prevent those of Sadiq Mahdi from undermining the cohesion of the NDA by fanning ethnic and religious sentiments among pan-Arabists and Islamists in Libya, Egypt and the Sudan. Garang was out to practically demonstrate his capability to bring the war to the North for Islamists to accept a realistic peace, rather than war. That strategic offensive was not undertaken to "kill Southern Sudanese children in the deserts of Northern Sudan" as claimed by some Southern leaders in opposition and renegades, who had Khartoum's support. Gains and losses accruing from SPLA incursion to the region that was part of the traditional North had been soberly evaluated and the positives were found to offset the negatives It was waged to save the people from what they experienced in 1991 after the split of the SPLM/A and even more.

In his capacity as the commander in chief of the SPLA, Dr John Garang took command of the third and final battle of Jekou, which saw the garrison fall to us in June1987. After the fall of the garrison to the SPLA, Garang succeeded in tricking the SAF command to send a helicopter to the periphery of Jekou garrison to rescue their escaping commander, Lieutenant Colonel Salim Saeid. The SAF sent a military helicopter to pick up the commander and the few soldiers who had fled with him. As the craft was about to land, one of the men on board—a Nuer member of pro-government Anya Nya—noted that the colleagues they were to pick up included enemies (SPLA). In the blink of an eye, the pilot changed course by lifting the craft skyward. The SPLA gunners immediately fired at the helicopter, which burst into a fireball. But one of their renegades on board knew a cousin among the SPLA forces and knew they were in an imminent ambush. That man shouted immediately to the pilot to take off and the pilot responded and left. Unexpectedly, the SPLA lost a helicopter that could be described as a valuable gift from the SAF. Within the SPLA ranks, there were officers who had received training to fly helicopters and other military aircraft.

Garang directed the battle for Pibor and had it liberated in 1987. He commanded the last attack on Nasir which fell to us in 1988. He was also in charge of the second and final assault on Kapoeta and won in 1989, and that was followed by the successful assault on Torit in 1989, which was followed in a matter of days by the capture of Bor, Ayod and Wat. A year later, Garang was at the helm during the battles for the liberation of entire Western Equatoria- Yambio, Lirongo, Sakure, Nabiapai, Nzara, Diabio, Naandi, Source Yubo, Mupoi, Tombura, Nagero to Rafili and threatened Wau in 1990. Also, under Garang's command, Maridi and Mundri fell to the SPLA in 1991. After forces under Cdr Salva Kiir took Kaya, Morobo, Lainya, Yei and Kajo Keji, in early 1997, Garang took part in the capture of Rumbek, Tonj, Warrap, Yirol and Mundri in 1997, when SAF forces at Bow decided to withdraw, afraid of the huge and gallant SPLA force which was advancing towards Bahr el Ghazal. The SPLA fighters also had the additional advantage of being familiar with the terrain and the population they were moving through in the manner of fish in water. The government army was fighting a losing war because of these factors as well as the high morale of the SPLA soldiers.

All the way, Garang depended on able officers he had coached over time, trained in his headquarters. Among his notable students and able commanders were: Oyay Deng Ajak, Bior-Aswad Ajang Duot, James Hoth Mai, Obote Mete Mamur, Anyar Apieu, Majok Mach Aluong, the late Pierre Ohure Okerruk, Gier Chuang Aluong and

Pieng Deng Kuol, among others. By training one means to follow very carefully, understand and practically do like Garang would do, in terms of command, and how one related to those under him. Next to Garang at the apex of the movement were Cdr Salva Kiir, Cdr Yousif Kuwa and Cdr Kuol Manyang, who had distinguished themselves in successful military operations. To be with Garang during operations, was like being in a typical classroom. And that was how he trained the officers who were around him, by example. To be responsible, alert, responsive, considerate, brave, active, simple and cooperative. Most of the surviving officers who were at the commander in chief's headquarters have now developed and qualified in studies and some were on the verge of completing their master's degree courses at the time these lines were being written.

Garang narrowly escaped death when a bullet missed him, when attacking Jekou in 1986. He also escaped death when they happened to hit a landmine, which bruised him in the head, coming from Ikotos near Heyala in a Soviet-made Ural truck. Near Renzi, he was narrowly missed by an air bomb with Cdrs Oyay, Hoth and Malik Agar when we were advancing to Yambio. For Garang, that was not to be the end of the struggle, but the essence of struggle. Winning battles in war never meant having achieved what we wanted. Winning a battle was only a means to achieve what we came to achieve on the table during peace talks under his leadership.

****

Before his comrades, Garang never denied a mistake. He would logically explain what had gone wrong and how it would be rectified or avoided in future. He did not advocate punitive action nor did he demand an apology to be made for mistakes that were judged to be unavoidable. Garang always believed that a comrade, a person with whom one shared the same vision and freely offered himself for the liberation of others, deserved to be treated humanely. A comrade would deserve to be trusted and share humane treatment of everyone including prisoners of war. The SPLM/A proved that by action since the SPLA spared the lives of the government soldiers captured in battle, unlike the SAF that did not apply the same principle.

25

SPLA Incursion into Western Equatoria

On our long triumphant advance to West Equatoria Region from November 1990 to March1991, Garang was with us all the way to Nzara and then returned to liberate Maridi. He commanded the whole campaign. For more than seventy miles, our route followed the bushy elephant grass broken terrain of the Nile-Congo Water Divide, marching like a trail of ants, where no forces of either of the two governments, Zaire and Sudan, existed on both sides of the border. We walked the water divide for half an hour and rested for an hour, for more than one hundred and twenty-five miles between Uele and Nabanga, passing under a canopy of shadow that stretched for more than ten miles between Ras Ulu and Kukudu.

Our force was big and in full operation mode, fully prepared to face any eventuality. At Kukudu, about 30 miles south of Maridi on the Sudan Zaire border, Garang sent for me. I left my comrades: A/Cdr Oyay Deng, A/Cdr James Hoth, A/Cdr Mayom Deng Biar and Lieutenant Luka Biong and others. We were about to relax under our armoured personnel carriers (APC) by the bridge. We were taking tea and smoking local tobacco rolled in a paper improvised from tender leaves. Lieutenant Luka Biong, under A/Cdr Mayom Deng Biar, led that small force, which advanced to secure Kukudu Bridge the night before. I dashed to meet Garang without delay.

After I saluted him, he promptly asked me about the overall situation of rations, since I was commanding the advancing force. I told him we had about ten bags of dry maize left and that was all.

He pondered as he focused on me and asked, "About ten sacks for more than six thousand comrades? Is that what you mean?" He was silent for a few moments before he told me, "Okay, and why are you bringing me this food? Do you want me to eat when the forces are starving? No!"

He did not touch the meal. I had no choice but to call in one of his guards to take the food, which he did, although reluctantly.

Then Garang passed me a list and ordered me to call in six NCOs all from the Zande nationality, by their individual names. Those members of the force were to be paraded outside his makeshift shelter for commissioning as officers, later to be transferred to different battalions followed by deployment. The integration of the newly-minted fighters amongst the advancing forces was positively received all over Western Equatoria; the residents were so delighted to find their sons taking charge as they communicated in their mother tongue, Zande language.

During their commissioning, I stood alongside Garang as he addressed them, saying, "Now you all know why I sent for you. Do not think that we have forgotten you all the time you were among us. You are our comrades. I was waiting for this day, and I am, indeed, happy that this day has come. Today onward you will all be promoted to become officers." Then he stood and ordered me to bring the badges and that I should dress them all. "From now onwards you are [commissioned] officers. Comrade Edward will brief you further."

I then marched them out, introduced them to their new assignments and then sent them to the units to which they had been transferred.

Present within the forces numbering more six thousand soldiers was First Lieutenant Oliver Duku, the only Zande from Ibba. The presence of the SPLA forces in there without officers from the area would have made us look like an occupation force. Those promotions greatly helped the movement in dispelling a potential perception. Garang had discussed the issue with me in my capacity as the campaign political officer when we were at Tore, where the campaign was launched before we departed a day earlier in the afternoon on November 21, 1990, to the Congo-Nile Water Divide on our advance towards Yambio, when I was ordered by the commander in chief to command our forces.

We marched on towards Nabanga, which was the only police outpost in the whole area. As I was the one leading the march, I was provided with a map. It was an old map on which the route to Nabanga was indicated to the east of the present route leading from Nabanga to the interior of Congo. I asked the local people, and they advised me to take the route leading westward, where there was a rivulet which flows between where we were and Nabanga. That map was drawn probably in the mid-1930s. The distance between the old road and the new one was about twenty miles.

We were trotting the highlands of the Congo-Nile Water Divide through an average rainforest. Changes in the terrain over the years should be expected. That same evening, I failed to reach Garang to inform him about the change in our route, because their radio was closed, which meant they were on the march. So, I decided to advance westward. When Garang came following me, he found that I had not followed the passage which was indicated on the map, and they got stuck in the mud. He was geared into anger by what he took as a grave mistake committed by me. Garang urgently sent a runner after me while the vehicle I was in got stuck in the mud for more than two hours on my new route. Although he was concerned, he took the incident as a passing cloud.

When I reached him, I found that he had sent Cdr James Hoth to find the same route at night, which was indicated on the map, searching with torches and hurricane lamps. When they returned, they found me standing to attention before Garang, and telling him what the people had told me: that the route I was taking was changed a long time before, meaning that there was a marshy all-season river flowing across the route and that there was no way for our vehicles—small and heavy, including armoured personnel carriers (APCs)—to cross. I was proven to have been right.

The point I need to record here was that I have never witnessed John Garang in that angry mood, since I came to know the man over the years, even before the SPLM came into being. He rebuked me severely, although his tone had no hint of bitterness. Disappointed as I was, I began to ask myself, *Really, what mistake have I committed? What has happened to him? Could it have been a result of hypertension or what could it be?* There were those rhetorical questions for which I had no definite answers.

I should add that while Garang was upset with me over the wrong route the vehicles took, for which he blamed me, he was mindful not to let others pick up what he was telling me. He always protected the privacy and dignity of others regardless of their ranks or social status.

To myself, I concluded that he must have been taken by anxiety to reach Nabanga as fast as possible, since our forces were exhausted and almost starving, a situation that worried us. In fact, there is nothing worse than to be under a commander who did not care about the welfare of his forces, especially when it comes to the issue of food. There was nothing that we could do to find food for the forces, a cardinal responsibility of any commander worth the name. For my part, however, I knew I was innocent in the situation we were in, although Garang had reprimanded me over the route the vehicles had taken and that caused the problem.

Soon after the liberation of Nabanga, the following evening we constructed a strong bridge on a small but deep twisting spring in an 'S' shape, on our route to the post. That bridge was hurriedly constructed under the directives of Said Kachu. A/Cdr Bior-Aswad Ajang and Lieutenant Atem Garang Dau, with bodyguards of the commander in chief, made our day. They flared off the police from the station in Nabanga in less than a quarter of an hour. I was met by Garang upon my arrival at Nabanga. He told me he "meant business", in reference to the event of the previous day. Since he was my boss I must obey, and I received without grumbling what was in fact a reprimand.

At Nabanga, we were pleasantly surprised to find the place had plenty of food. There we stumbled on sixty barrels, all full to the brim with pure natural honey. Nabanga produced abundant varieties of foods and many kinds of fruits. At midnight we heard chickens clucking and knew that there were comrades there, who were about to prepare a special meal. That was the only time in which Garang was able to have a meal, since we left Kukudu. Since we were very happy for our swift victory and our forces were all in a celebration mood, Garang sent Richard Mulla, Mayom Deng Biar and me, a bottle of whisky (Red Label) in the light drizzling rain. We had to celebrate that night, happy for the fall of Nabanga and our entry into our country from the Congo. When Garang was about to resort to bed after midnight he borrowed my pillow and that alerted us about his need to rest. It had been an exceptionally hectic day, but victorious.

In Nabanga we were all summoned by Garang at about 10:00 in the morning. He handed us charts, Commanders Oyay Deng, James Hoth, Mayom Deng, Richard K. Mulla, Majok Mach, Malik Agar, Dr Monywiir Arop Kuol, Justice Monyluak Alor and myself. The commander in chief allocated to each of us specific assignments for the attack and capture of Yambio government garrison. A/Cdr Bior-Aswad Ajang was ordered to head towards Ibba to contain Maridi from the west. Our missions were to liberate Ibba, Yambio, Nzara,

Naandi, Ezzo and Source Yubo, Mupoi, Tombura and Bou Bridge. Garang decided to join our mission. At midday A/Cdr Bior (Aswad) Ajang led his forces towards Ibba and we marched to Yambio. At about midnight we heard guns from behind us and we knew Bior had begun to attack Ibba, and we marched on towards Yambio.

As we were about to cross Sue Bridge, we stumbled into a light ambush, which we overran. Minutes later, we were informed that Bior had captured Ibba. We were excited for that quick victory. We overran Bazingau, a small outpost and advanced throughout the night. Garang caught us up near Renze where his entourage was narrowly missed by bombs from the air. As we marched to Bazingwe, closer to Yambio, we fell into the second ambush, but towards evening we overran it. We then rested before we marched in two files into Yambio.

We liberated Yambio at midnight and advanced to Nzara walking in two euphoric files. Brigadier Isaiah Paul was reported to be in Nzara. He had once fallen into our ambush at Tore-Wande near Kajo Keji, but escaped our capture in a lady's dress, so this news about him was very spicy and we moved to capture him. Nzara is sixteen miles from Yambio. We took some rest along the way and arrived at Nzara at about 10:00 am and found the town empty. The enemy forces had withdrawn towards Source Yubo and Tambura. We inspected the whole town and found no trace of them. I went to where Brigadier Isaiah Paul was accommodated and found wet slippers and hot tea in a flask. Isaiah had gone. The guards and I occupied his house, and after a while, Oyay Deng Ajak came and took the next room. We had to rest because we had not slept for three days.

That same evening, as we were inspecting the ginning and soap factory of Nzara with A/Cdr Mayom Deng Biar, we linked up with Garang's entourage entering Nzara. Garang stopped amidst the euphoria of men congratulating themselves for all the success achieved in the clearing of Nabanga, Bazingau, Rimenze, Bazigino,

Yambio, Lirongo, Nzara and Ibba in a matter of three days. The following day, Garang sent for me. It was a glorious moment.

Before the meeting started, I informed Garang of the presence of General (retired) Samuel Abu John in the vicinity of Sakure, to confirm what Cdr Malik Agar sent to him in a message from Yambio. Immediately, he picked up a pen to send a handwritten message to Uncle Samuel Abu John in which he mentioned an event known only to the two of them, and which occurred during the Anya Nya days, when they were in the Congo. Cdr Malik Agar, who was appointed Civil Military Administrator of Yambio County, dispatched an officer, Lieutenant Edward Sebit to bring General Samuel Abu John to Yambio to attend the public briefing, which Garang was about to hold in Yambio and happily, Samuel Abu John attended.

The next morning, Cdr Oyay Deng and I decided to join our forces on their way northward to clear Naandi, Ezo and Source Yubo and converge with Cdr James Hoth and Cdr Majok Mach in Tambura and northward. Hence, we left earlier in the morning before Garang could be informed, as planned. Garang wanted me to join him to start organising how to "run our new liberated areas", since Richard K. Mulla was still behind in Nabanga.

Upon our return from Tombura, the first thing he told me was that all the areas had been captured intact with their civil administration in place. Garang spoke at length about the importance of involving our Azande people by empowering them in the administration of the liberated areas and to join the movement to strengthen the defence of their rights. It took us time to chart new administrative boundaries of the liberated areas and rename them as counties instead of previous districts. So, Yambio was declared by Garang to be the first county in all the liberated areas in 1990. Comrade Richard Mulla arrived and together we went to form Tambura County followed by Maridi then Mundri. From there, we met Cdr Daniel Awet Akot who came specifically from Bahr el Ghazal to meet us and see how counties were formed and administered in the new civil administrative entities not subjected to the SPLA.

When we arrived, we met Garang at Nzara. We were driving a long convoy of a total of 48 vehicles from Source Yubo. We entered Bambuti on the other side of our international borders with Central Africa Republic, where people from Yambio and Tombura had fled to, afraid of our advance. They tried to flee in vehicles to Central African Republic (CAR). After catching up with them we ordered them to hand over to us all the fleeing government soldiers together with all the weapons they had used. These orders included the return of all the vehicles they had taken and used for their failed attempt to drive to CAR.

After our long negotiations with the representatives from CAR, they agreed to hand over to us all the vehicles. During our communication with the CAR authorities, we had given ourselves pseudonyms: with Cdr Oyay Deng going by General Gordon, Cdr James Hoth as General Peters, while I presented myself as General Lino.

What was strange in the mission we had assumed was that we kept Garang, in his capacity as the SPLM chairman and the SPLA commander in chief, in the dark about our illegal incursion into CAR. We knew if we told him about the mission, he would veto it since it was a blatant violation of the sovereignty of another nation. We only informed him after our overnight operation was over, having retrieved more than the 40 vehicles, which we drove to Nzara, and he was extremely happy. He had been worried when he failed to encounter any one of us online for the whole day and night. When we narrated to him our adventure into the Central African Republic without his permission, Garang joked, saying that had we failed in executing the daring mission he would have flayed us alive. We all laughed.

We found Garang with a new group of revolutionary guests from Darfur in a meeting. It was great to meet them with Garang. He introduced them to us, starting from Daoud Bolaad. The group had come all the way to meet Garang driving from Addis Ababa to Nzara through the bush, a distance of not less than 3250 kilometres, during the third week of December 1990. Our guests were excited with our triumphant arrival. Garang wanted to know from Dawood Bolaad—previously one of the core Islamist student leaders at the University of Khartoum and considering that he was then out to fight the Islamist-oriented regime—what made them undertake such an unprecedented journey from Addis Ababa to Nzara in less than a week.

Dawood's response was "Indeed, I have been fighting you for long. But when I started to weigh blood and religion, I came to conclude that blood was thicker than religious affiliation."

To me, that answer hit the nail on the head; he was correct as far as the system of rule in Sudan was concerned because often in the Sudanese context fellow Muslims of Arab descent treated each other as more equal than fellow Muslims from non-Arab racial groups. We rose to embrace our new comrades in arms.

With the fresh arrival of the group direct from Addis Ababa, we saw the possibility of advancing to Darfur. But that needed some preparations, which took about a year. That came to be undertaken towards the second half of 1991. I happened to be given the responsibility of delivering ammunition to Cdr Abel Aziz Adam Hilu, required for his long advance to Darfur. His advance was very hectic and had never been attempted before from the Zande land. It ended as one of the most tragic journeys, in which we lost Dawood Bolaad, Deng Mior and other comrades in Darfur. The contingent for that dangerous mission was commanded by the gallant Cdr Abdel Aziz Adam Al Hilu.

The swift liberation of Yambio gave the movement a golden chance to speed up the "separation of civil administration from military administration", as an important stage of transforming the movement to set a powerful political organisation, the SPLM, to guard the civil life of our people and direct the army, SPLA, after years of being the one leading the struggle. Garang knew SPLA was the one dominating administration in all the liberated areas and knew the negative impact that reality had on the general performance of the army and how they imposed themselves on the civil population. Let alone the dissatisfaction of the civil population with the way in which they were being administered in a manner that was very demanding and Garang was aware of that, and he began to change it.

SPLM did not exist on the ground, as a matter of fact. But it captured the heart of every SPLA member. Our people feared to talk about the SPLA, primarily because they were not organised. That riddle hampered the rapid growth of the movement and negatively affected its presence among the people. Given the high rate of illiteracy in the countryside among peasants and the dominance of the few educated elite atop the movement, it was so difficult to spread political awareness among the people with the rate of prevailing poverty in Southern Sudan, the Nuba Mountains and Blue Nile with no schools.

27

Impediments in the Bush

Some readers might enquire, why the SPLM, being a popular movement with a rich experience in the countryside and in the cities for years, did not assert itself to be a leading political party. Thus, examining the facts to which the movement was exposed, one would find two main impediments. One of these was that the number of comrades who reported for enrolment in the movement, did that from isolated areas with previous attempts to organise their "political aspirations", although they were not ideologically or organisationally uniform. The other point was that almost all the recruits reported "primarily for military training to confront the Sudanese army in their devastated villages". Political training, therefore, was something secondary to them.

Before the movement emerged, there were more than six groups, which designated to themselves the label "movement", in Southern Sudan and the Nuba mountains. One of these was "Anya Nya Two." They were independent from one another. Each of them was blocked in an isolated locality from which it derived supporters. And because of the way they were haphazardly organised to protect civilians from the Sudan army, it became hard to redeem new recruits from doing what the Sudanese army was doing to civilians led by intelligentsia. Lack of appropriate experience attracted them to copy what the enemy was doing to the civil population, and that approach became the way they treated civilians. It was apparent that in a situation lacking conscious leadership, inappropriate and repulsive habits could creep in, and lawlessness became the norm, factors that could alienate the civilian inhabitants where armed groups operate.

The SPLM/A rose to exert discipline in the liberated areas. A disciplinary law was produced and passed to regulate relations within the movement as well as with the civil population in the theatre of war and the SPLA members. The laws spelt out specific penalties for offences such as rape, and armed robbery committed against civilians and their properties. The laws included provisions for the protection of the environment, particularly wildlife species deemed to face extinction.

The vast land, including much uninhabited plain or thick forest, lacks reliable all-weather roads. This creates problems for transport and communication. During the war, movement of recruits from their home areas, most of which were very far from the SPLA bases, was one of the difficulties that faced recruits, especially after their training and deployment to theatres of fighting. Throughout the areas where fighters were deployed to homeland fronts, communities through which the SPLA forces had to pass, local volunteers that included womenfolk would assist the soldiers with the carriage of ammunition crates or other heavy military equipment, which would be relayed to the inhabitants of the next village, and the process would be repeated until the destination would be reached.

The kind of impediments mentioned earlier played a negative role in the job of moulding recruits in the various training centres. One of these factors was the many languages other than Arabic and English, spoken by many of the recruits, rendering communication between the recruits and their instructors difficult, as well as among the recruits themselves. The harsh climatic conditions and a diet often inadequate and poor in nutrition caused considerable deaths at the training centres.

In addition to military training, political orientation was made an integral component of the course. The necessity of teaching political awareness was dictated by the awareness that a fighter lacking political objectives was bound to embrace militarism as a doctrine, a deviation that was a negation of the objectives of the political struggle that used armed struggle purely for political ends. That was the main obstacle Garang faced when he attempted to transform the movement. He was quite aware of the problems people were facing and to handle each of them pointing at a different reality with which to deal. Not separately, but synchronised to create harmony nationwide, when resolving a national problem. But Garang left us before handling that basic organisational obstacle, being the founding father.

28

Time for Relaxation

Garang always knew how to spend his time. When idle on a journey he played cards, dominoes, chess, read something light, went hunting or swimming in an open river. He would sneak away for short entertainment, to meet new acquaintances and so forth. But Garang never had women for his entertainment, as far as we know. In Pan-Anyang near Nasir he collected the four of us, Oyay Deng, James Hoth, Gier Chuang and me and the guards to join him in swimming in the Sobat River. We plunged ourselves into Sobat for about two hours of swimming.

When SPLA was opening a new road from Mizan Tafari in southwestern Ethiopia to Boma, they wanted to have some meat. So, he offered himself to hunt. People in need would rarely differentiate what they wanted. He brought them zebra. When the meal was prepared everyone knew they were going to take zebra meat.

When Kerubino Kuanyin tried to refuse eating under the pretext that he could not eat what he considered to be a donkey, Garang instantly intervened saying, "Who told you that this is a donkey? This is zebra. Eat, eat just as I am doing." Kerubino had no choice, but to follow the example set by his boss.

John Garang met almost all the chiefs, notables and elders in the areas he went taking notes. Through them, he was kept informed about cultures and livelihood of the people. Garang took notes as he socialised and spoke attentively to them and would pass by them whenever he was nearby as a normal thing, which a caring leader should do. In 2004 and before the conclusion of the Comprehensive Peace Agreement, Garang de Mabior staged one of the most memorable "consultative conferences" ever held in the history of modern Sudan.

He invited almost all the chiefs from the South, the Nuba Mountains and Southern Blue Nile to brief them about the peace process and took them on board before the signing of the CPA. Garang had to seek their opinions and support in a democratic way. That conference was vital to him, because Garang took them to be the representatives and spokespersons of the people who must be duly informed and whose consent was of vital importance in the peace process, as the legitimate beneficiaries of peace. The kings, chiefs and notables who were against the movement had all escaped to the north and to Khartoum. Those who remained deserved to be informed about what their movement was doing.

Garang took that historic week as an ideal occasion to thank all the kings, chiefs, tribal leaders and notables for the contributions they offered throughout the long years of the struggle. Eventually, he took that golden chance and sincerely stood before the conference to apologise on behalf of the movement, SPLM/A, for every unfortunate mishap, which took place during the war. That was what he meant, to be always with the people and work with the people, for the people. He briefed them openly and implored for their forgiveness. With tears, the conference received his apology.

He then asked for their consent, telling them, "If you do not agree, then we cannot go ahead." He explained to them the importance of their agreement to bring peace.

Now how did Garang invite and transport more than five hundred kings, chiefs and notables from remote villages of about half of Sudan to New Site in the southeastern corner of Southern Sudan? They came to meet, intermingle and come to know each other with the leadership of the movement and among themselves for the first time in the history of Sudan. Could that be an act of a dictator? Now, can we follow those giant strides with the sense of commitment to our revolution that inspired us to embrace inclusivity? That historic conference, no doubt, bestowed legitimacy to the movement.

Garang would never let idleness kill his time. He spent his time wisely in a proper way. He had always controlled his movements. Garang loved listening to jokes and sometimes made his own, often laced with biting humour. To him, witty jokes were like a breath of fresh air. Without jokes, laughter or smiles, boredom takes over. A person facing serious disappointments, gloom, sickness, privation from life's basic needs such as hunger, anger, thirst, destitution, loneliness, or when facing an upsetting situation such as sadness, heart-breaking news daily and around the clock, is bound to aggravate existing health concerns such as hypertension, for instance. On the other hand, jokes can alleviate stressful situations.

Garang has left us a handful of jokes, which can be recalled at a later time. He cracked humorous anecdotes, especially when confronted by an upsetting or hostile situation, and he rarely showed or expressed irritation, going to the extent of relishing negative statements, outright lies or absurdities hurled at him by his adversaries.

As far as I can recall, I never had a chance to hear Garang belittling, shunning or being impolite to any person of any social standing. There was one person, however, who was the exception: that one man, whom he avoided for obvious reasons: Ishaq Ahmed Fadlallah, to avoid being wrongly portrayed! About people in general he said, "No one would know, if the person one shuns or insults turns out to be a friend, an acquaintance or someone with whom one might take an assignment, what would you do? Garang respected people. He welcomed people and thanked them for whatever they contributed.

29

Garang and the World of Ideas

Sudan, according to Garang, was a unique situation with diverse historical and social complexities, cultural and religious especially, with which to deal. And he did it diligently. He studied history, to see the correctness of our path. He extensively read the collections of UNESCO (United Nations Educational, Scientific and Cultural Organization) about the history of the Nile Valley by Professor Cheikh Anta Diop, the Senegalese historian. And he discovered areas of great interest in our history, which should help to rebuild the Sudan, if our people were truthful to abide by the realities of the history of the Nile Valley.

Garang extensively read the Bible and found himself in it, as a person born along a section of River Gihon, like the one mentioned in the Bible. Flowing from the land of Cush where South Sudan is never far today. He studied ancient Egyptian history and Sudan and compared them. He was an extensively read intellectual. Hence, the difference between Garang and other intellectuals was his commitment to observing the things that would impact on the wellbeing of his people.

The main difference between him and some of his colleagues was how he dealt with problems in an objective transparent manner. Some of them were mere armchair intellectuals who would encounter wrongs being committed, but would consider them preordained happenings, which must be taken as facts of life. He was not an opportunistic or a cowardly person. Garang was always steady and daring, unlike other intellectuals who do not endeavour to contribute what could change lives for the better.

All the wars in past centuries were directed southward against our ancestors until today. Our gains could be great and monumental, if we defend them and show the younger generation how to protect our gains. But if we happen to mishandle our trust and lose the thrust, then this young generation would be the last generation to live in this part of the globe. This is the biggest trust our people should never lose. This breathing space we enjoy today, is what Garang was able to contribute to us. With a history that dates to prehistoric times, this is where our people should rise and assert ourselves anew among nations.

30

Inside the Movement

The darkest moment in the entire history of the SPLM/A after the 1991 schism was the sharp difference that rose between Cdr Salva Kiir and Garang from July to September 2004. The meeting in Rumbek succeeded to contain the differences that were threatening to tear us apart and destroy the gains of the political and armed struggle. The differences were partly a result of unfounded stories circulating from both sides, which blew into a crisis that almost threatened a bloody confrontation between the two leaders. Allegations reached Salva Kiir asserting that Garang had decided "to arrest him and replace him with Nhial Deng Nhial". But there was no truth to that claim. It was a concoction by some individuals who were unhappy with Garang. That story was exploited by some individuals, who were hostile to Garang's leadership. Those included elements with ties to Government of Sudan and its intelligence branch, all bent on derailing the peace efforts in Kenya. Luckily, the tension was amicably resolved peacefully.

The move demonstrated how the two parties were concerned about the importance of the unity of purpose within the movement at all levels, from the grassroots to the top leadership. And that was the reason they decided to meet and present their differences to comrades. Peace by then was about four months to be concluded in Naivasha, Kenya. That was, indeed, a noble move. The leadership of the movement and senior officers went to Rumbek to attend that meeting. The situation seemed to be tense, but the reality was that most of the SPLA officers and men who were in Rumbek by then took no side in the conflict. Their interest was only peace, through one united movement under one united leadership.

In Rumbek, some of us had very incriminating reports about Khartoum's intention to foil the peace process by igniting an upheaval or what was described as an "internal coup" against Garang. There was also talk among certain circles, at home and within the international community, expressing concern if both Garang and Kiir were to leave the leadership of the SPLM/A to other Southern Sudanese. Our concern was the wellbeing of the masses of our people and the future of the movement. That was the main objective of the people of Southern Sudan, and we wanted the SPLM to stand solidly united as a movement under the leadership of Garang, with Kiir as his first deputy.

During the Rumbek meeting, arguments, accusations and counteraccusations and conciliatory appeals dominated the deliberations. Sessions began in the evening and would grind on to early morning hours, for three full days. The news of a happy ending, with reconciliation between the two colleagues, was signalled by hoisting the movement's banner aloft the rooftop of a building for the public to see that all was then well with their vanguard movement and its leadership. From Rumbek our delegates immediately flew to Nairobi to conclude the CPA. Outside the corridors of the meeting room, numerous adversaries, who detested the happy ending, were anxiously waiting for bursts of heavy gunfire to signal death of some comrades and an end to our unity of ranks. Khartoum did not sleep the night we concluded our meetings when Garang and Kiir warmly embraced amidst rapturous cheers and ululations of our mothers, wives and sisters all over Rumbek and beyond.

That meeting was highly infiltrated by Khartoum, which had sent agents who were conveying whatever went on through telephones relayed directly from loudspeakers, which were blaring throughout the normally quiet nights of Rumbek. It was strange that the meetings were orchestrated and made public. Several agents working for Khartoum were conspicuously scattered in and outside the venue, confirming what was said by Garang during the graduation of Shield Five (officers' batch) at Bonga, in 1988, when told the cadets that the SPLM/A had learned how to swim in turbulent waters, by which he meant that although the enemy would be able to encircle us, no obstacle should stop our march to victory. On that day in Rumbek, we triumphantly marched for unity within our ranks and the achievement of the goals we had set for ourselves.

That was the message, how the new era of the movement came to be. We witnessed how the leadership reconciled and proceeded to undertake their duties up to the time Garang died. On his return to Rumbek from Khartoum Garang, now the First Vice President of the Republic and the President of the Government of South Sudan, made it known publicly that he had appointed Salva Kiir to be his deputy for the Government of Southern Sudan, because he trusted him as his comrade and an orphaned brother with whom he survived all the years of the struggle. And he added: Salva Kiir was fully empowered to administer the South, since he would be paying attention to what he described as important issues to be tackled in Khartoum.

In the first meeting of the members of the SPLM/A Leadership Council, when Cdr Salva Kiir recalled them to that emergency meeting at New Site after the death of John Garang on August 1, 2005, Garang's remains were awaiting transportation to Juba for interment. During that emergency, the leaders who had gathered there unanimously designated Cdr Salva Kiir to succeed John Garang, to the surprise of the world and the relief of patriotic Southern Sudanese, because there was an extensive fear that Garang's loss would create a vacuum and potential rivalries for succession within the movement. Kiir did not assume the leadership of the movement by means of a coup, as some people tend to believe today. Besides Kiir, there was not even a single member from his Bahr el Ghazal region to cast a vote for him. Kiir was selected to succeed Garang because he was the second in command to Garang. There was no valid reason to block him as Garang's successor. The democratic process installed Cdr Salva Kiir as the chairman of the SPLM as well as the commander in chief of the SPLA. That empowerment was followed by elections in the Second SPLM Convention in Juba, 2008. The convention confirmed him as the chairman of the SPLM and commander in chief of the SPLA for the following four years, until people decided otherwise in a general election. That was what our people were aspiring for: orderly, democratic and peaceful transfer of power. So far, so good.

****

A few days after General Salva Kiir had ascended to the helm of SPLM/A and assumed the position of the First Vice President of the Republic, some people who happened to be his kin and kith, began to demonstrate puzzling behaviours: open hostility and harassment to most of the personnel they found in Garang's office. There was a case of young fellows within the entourage of First Vice President Salva Kiir, who told the former staff of the late Garang to vacate their positions for them on the basis that their "role in the office of Salva Kiir was over".

In Juba, elements who happened to be kin to the new leader, were observed to be moving closer to the presidential residence. It was common knowledge that after sunset those self-appointed guardians would ferry messages sealed in congratulatory messages to the new leader in addition to other reports about who was not to be trusted or watched with care and so forth.

Before the arrest and detention of Cdr Kerubino Kuanyin in 1987, Garang had wanted his two colleagues, William Nyuon Bany and Salva Kiir to be trained in Cuba, but unfortunately, some people misunderstood the objective of the plan, going as far as to claim that it was Garang's plot to exile his colleagues. That baseless account was wildly circulating in Itang refugee camp, which at the time was home to thousands of refugees from Southern Sudan, who were not only members of the SPLM; many of the SPLA fighters had their parents there.

In 1988, after meeting a DUP delegation in Addis Ababa, Cdr Abdel Aziz Adam Hilu and I accompanied Cdr Lam Akol to report to Garang about the outcome of the meeting, which was welcomed by people in Khartoum. Abdel Aziz went to meet him on a different mission. Garang was at that time in Hilieu near Heyala. From Addis Ababa to Hilieu not far from Torit was a long distance that took us about four hectic days. In Hilieu and after the meeting, Garang sent for me in the evening to join him for dinner. He talked to me about the importance of supporting Cdr William Nyuon and Cdr Salva Kiir and do the best we could and not to let them be frustrated by adversaries, according to what he had gathered.

At that time there were self-seeking individuals out to win over some senior commanders to their side by trying to mislead them against Garang and some progressive members in the movement, when in fact, Garang had nothing of that sort against his comrades. I told Garang about how best to help them to learn, by giving them short study courses in neighbouring countries like Tanzania, where they could be inducted into political theories and practice, to be given field visits to some branches of the ruling party there to gain practical knowledge. There and then, I left Garang without discussing that matter again. The most important point to note, was the concern Garang had about the future of his two colleagues who were not ready to be exposed to education to enrich their knowledge of public affairs. They were both blindfolded by their positions in the movement and the influence of those who lied to them about the proposed training outside Southern Sudan.

Salva Kiir was a remarkable intelligence officer, fluent in English and Arabic. He was also competent at analysis and understanding matters related to intelligence or the political situation. Cdr Salva Kiir was a man endowed with strong human feelings, which stood in contradiction to the way he became in his last days corrupted by power. Throughout his life and before he was taken to the other extreme by obduracy, the man was extremely intelligent. For instance, when the Ethiopian rebels of EPRDF ousted Mengistu Haile Mariam from power, the movement and its personnel left Ethiopia, leaving documentations behind, most of them in Bilpam. The only person who was there and who remembered the names of officers in the movement by heart was none other than Cdr Salva Kiir. He remembered all the batches by name and even seniority, nearly all who had trained under his personal supervision.

In his seclusion, heavy storms could gather in his mind, scatter his thinking and drive him into obstinacy. For instance, he hated Dr Riek Machar for what he knew about him, of which his point of no return was his 1991 attempted coup for power, which turned him against the intelligentsia, especially the university graduates. Kiir was not happy with Garang when he decided to "reward" Riek Machar, rather than Cdr James Wani, with the position of second deputy chairman of the SPLM in 2000. That mistrust was the main cause for the rift, which led him to drift from Garang and the people he suspected to be closer to Garang.

But now Kiir had burned his boat in a journey of no return, perhaps to the North, when he told some of his colleagues that he was ready to "dismantle the country by breaking it, so that whoever wants to rule will find it impossible to govern". That was President Kiir in Juba talking in 2013 before three witnesses.

Almost all the SPLA officers and other people one met during the struggle liked Salva Kiir for his kindness as a person, gentility as a leader and toughness as a commander. As an officer he grew in prominence from the days of Anya Nya in the intelligence service to the days of the dictatorship of Jaafar Nimeiri, followed by the armed struggle in which he oversaw the intelligence branch. All those experiences transformed him to become ruthless as was demonstrated by the events of December 15, 2013, when fighting broke out in Juba and all over the country. One major weakness of President Kiir is that he listens wholeheartedly to unconfirmed reports and hearsay from sycophants.

In 1992 in a conference at Moya Sukhun in Equatoria, Cdr Salva Kiir, who was by then deputy leader of the SPLM/A, met over 250 intelligence officers who were under him at the time they had been deployed to the Nuba Mountains, Southern Sudan, Blue Nile and other combat zones. He was happy to meet them after an absence of about seven years. He stood to greet them one by one, and addressing each by his full name, and when he was doubting his memory he would say, "Either this, your father's name or the other." To the surprise of all who were listening, he was correct in remembering the full names of all the officers he was chatting with. The meeting stood up applauding in admiration and appreciation. Those people who abetted Cdr Salva Kiir in committing serious blunders later turned around to attribute the faults to John Garang.

31

A Monument to the Cause of Freedom

At the start of the SPLM/A Garang was deputised by personalities who could hardly distinguish between a people's revolution and warlordism. People were militaristically oriented since 1955 and even before that. Armed conflict was what they were used to since the days our people were facing the Turko-Egyptian occupation (1822 to 1884), the Condominium rule from 1898 to 1956, and the civil war from 1955 to 1972 and the recruitments, which followed their inclusion into the Sudan Defence Force with junior ranks. Illiteracy and lack of political consciousness were the two main hindrances facing the masses. Garang had to deal with this in his own way. As a concept, the SPLM was new to the majority of Southern Sudanese. Some men with formal education began to join SPLM/A at later periods, aspiring for leadership positions after July 1983, when the name and the movement's manifesto were published and released.

Some of those who had joined, were people either hunting for opportunities and positions of some influence or escaping from potential apprehension for various indictable offences they had committed. There were several varied motives, not directly linked to patriotism, accounting for some individuals who decided to join the inchoate rebel organisation. Garang was aware of those facts. For him, public education about the objectives of the movement would transform those with narrow selfish motives to committed freedom fighters. To him it was a matter of time when political education and the right orientation would transform members with such thinking into true agents of struggle for justice and equality for all. To Garang it was a matter of time until such transformation would occur, and what was required was patience, perseverance and belief in the correctness of the path the SPLM/A had charted.

As a leader who had little to offer to the volunteers by way of personal reward but sacrifice, Garang knew that the real reward for all the rank and file of the movement was the achievement of liberation, no matter how long the struggle would last.

Garang believed power struggle at that stage was a distraction that should not be allowed to drain the energy and the unity of all ranks required for the liberation struggle. Within a fleeting time Garang performed to the best of his ability to turn all positive aspects in our people into unchallengeable strength directed towards achieving freedom. Most of the people went on without knowing or understanding how the SPLM/A was moving united in harmony. But Garang took all positive aspects in our people and turned them into a formidable patriotic endeavour.

John Garang deeply appreciated whatever our people offered to sustain our war effort. He taught and coached them all the way long, with unbendable dedication. As a matter of fact, those who differed from him at later dates did so, because they were people endowed with myopic vision. People who failed to know and understand how a leader should think, act or where a leader should go, were endowed with aimless agendas, which they failed to achieve.

Therefore, some people became impatient with the style of Garang's leadership and quit in disgrace. Twenty-two long years of resolute armed struggle was not a picnic and carrying weapons for that long was not a licence to loot the people. Garang faced tough times throughout the years, but he sailed through patiently and unbroken. He overcame acts of treason and betrayal from some of his colleagues who wanted quick fixes in a protracted armed struggle, but they prevailed, with some of the plots being nipped in the bud due to the vigilance of the people in their determination to protect their revolution.

Indeed, Dr John Garang de Mabior Atem lived as a model of a dedicated revolutionary, who was a forgiving leader, who was ready to forgive his detractors, except when they were out to undermine the people's quest for justice. It is worth noting that those wayward colleagues he often forgave for their transgression, did not even dare to thank him and forgive him in return.

He was a devoted family man. He once told me when he returned from Eritrea that Mabior, his eldest son, had gone for military training in the parched wilderness of Eastern Sudan. He added that the terrain was challenging, but he wanted his son to be trained there to later join the ranks of the rest of the patriots engaged in the struggle. Garang concluded by telling me that what we were carrying out in the cause of the liberation struggle, was not a joke, and that it would not be long before the outcome of what we were doing would be achieved and witnessed by all and that our children must know what we were doing. As a father, he was as proud as any other father would be for a son doing what is right.

Garang deeply loved his wife, Rebecca, and their children. In 1988 I met his two kids on their way to Hilieu to visit their father during their school vacation. At that time Mabior and Chol were over ten years old. Before that, their mother Rebecca had visited him in the field, unlike the wives of other members of the High Command. Whenever I reported to him at different times in Nairobi, Kampala, in the field or anywhere his family had visited him, I would retreat to another place to allow him to be alone with Rebecca, Gak (third daughter after Mabior and Chol), Kuir, Atong, Chol, Mabior or any member of his family.

It was heartening to see him with his family in an environment where ranks, or social standing had no place. At least the public figure that Garang was, had the right of privacy and to be allowed to bask in an environment not governed by hierarchy and its etiquette. For Garang, family life was one of sacred domains that everyone deserves to enjoy while its privacy must be protected because anyone engaged in a struggle should not be treated as a hermit.

John Garang was so considerate and open in all his dealings. To break the ice between the two, he availed himself to Ali Osman Mohamed Taha in Naivasha to the extent of introducing their families to one another, virtually an uncommon practice in many parts of the developing world, especially in African and Islamic context, where womenfolk are rarely allowed to interact with strangers. Garang was straightforward to the point he started to discuss those hot issues by cracking jokes to cool the atmosphere. He fully mastered the art of honouring even an adversary with heart-warming acts and jokes. Garang always took sufficient time to study opponents in order to obtain an appropriate strategy he would need in support of his stand or for disarming his opponents or to deflect likely assaults against him.

John Garang was a very humble person. He never presented himself as a highly educated person, who shuns those with modest credentials and from humble backgrounds. The proof of that was demonstrated in the way he tolerated the wayward behaviour of his immediate colleagues in the leadership: Kerubino Kuanyin Bol, William Nyuon Bany and Salva Kiir up to when each of them decided to take a different way. Garang sincerely respected them and never tried to humiliate or look down on them, when none of them measured up to him academically. When Cdr William Nyuon defected from the SPLM/A in Pageri area in 1992, he departed about midday when people were watching him withdrawing in panic and restlessness, after he was persuaded in a series of long, hectic meetings attended by Garang, Salva Kiir, Kuol Manyang, John Kong, Deng Alor, Oyay Deng and other senior commanders.

32

Nurturing Foreign Relations

Through his steady march, as the leader of the SPLM/A, Garang began our external relations virtually from the little we did in Khartoum with the Ethiopians and the Egyptians whom we kept informed about what was happening in Southern Sudan. That kept the Egyptians cautious whenever dealing with the Sudan the way we wanted. John Garang exerted tremendous efforts to build a strong diplomatic presence internationally, starting from Ethiopia, which Garang took to be strategic. He went to Libya, Cuba, South Yemen, Zimbabwe, Namibia, Uganda, Zaire (current Democratic Republic of Congo), Kenya, Egypt, Chad, Norway, USA, Germany, United Kingdom, Italy, South Africa and other countries.

Consciously, Africa being our home was decided to be our firm base from where to begin an extensive diplomatic assault on Khartoum. That was accomplished with remarkable success. From those warm friendly relations, we started with Ethiopia in particular, where we came to receive what made us known as a struggling people who deserved to be supported. Garang stood his ground and presented the distinctiveness of our case logically. Foreign relations were left for Garang with a few colleagues. The team consisted of

Riek Machar, Lam Akol, Martin Manyiel, Deng Alor, Justin Yach, Nhial Deng Nhial and a few others.

From Africa, the expanding relations of the movement took Garang across the Atlantic to Cuba, where President Fidel Castro of Cuba warmly received him. The Cubans welcomed the movement and agreed to offer military training and scholarships. The relation between Cuba and the SPLM/A was not welcomed by the State Department in Washington for several years after Mengistu was deposed. Garang was asked, why the movement should build ties with Cuba and whether he was a communist.

He responded by saying: "I am not a communist. I am a freedom fighter. And we have nobody helping us. The Cuban leadership willingly offered to help us by taking our children who had been deprived of education to learn free within their institutions of learning. If there were people to help us educate our children, then we have no objection with that, since Cuba is too far from us."

Many journalists and Middle Eastern columnists, both leftists and Islamists, who supported the governments in Khartoum and the Arab world in general, considered the movement as a new American tool set against the Arab and Islamic world in general and Sudan in particular. Some Western-oriented intellectuals took the SPLM for a new and dangerous communist tool in the heart of Africa directed by Mengistu Haile Mariam. That was precisely our situation towards the end of the cold war. But no journalist or writer spared time to come and see the movement, besides some swift reporters who ran after lights. In those days, except for America and Britain, no power was interested in what was going on in Southern Sudan and the whole Sudan for that matter, after Nimeiri turned to the West, until oil, a strategic commodity, was discovered in Sudan. For his part, Garang had the chance to look for means to sell our case regionally and of the people internationally in a manner that did not hinder the legitimate aspirations of the masses. One important contact we had in

Khartoum was to create friendly relations with the Egyptians. Since time immemorial, Egypt has been an important neighbour to Sudan. During our days, we came to understand that Sudan had a desk in the Presidency unlike the other countries whose affairs are handled by the Ministry of Foreign Affairs. It was that fact that encouraged us to seek friendship with Egypt. Through a retired senior Egyptian officer from Southern Sudan from the family of Jadein in Rumbek of Azande Dinka origin, we were introduced to Brigadier Emad, the Egyptian Consul General in Sudan. One was introduced also to Captain Ahmed Rajab and Lieutenant Mahmoud Abdel Khaliq.

In 1983, relations between Egypt and Sudan went through a bumpy turn when the movement was still young. We made it a point to confront the Egyptians with the fact that they always looked at Southern Sudan through Khartoum for being basically an allied Arabo-Islamic country. That perception was not acceptable to Southern Sudanese and the reality of the Nile Basin region. For our part, we told them the SPLM was ready to deal directly with Egypt because in our view there was no enmity between Southern Sudan and Egypt. Our Egyptian hosts warmly welcomed our position and agreed to deal with the SPLM through the Presidency like the status they accorded to Sudan as a sovereign country. Since 1983, SPLM began to put Egypt in the picture about what authorities in Khartoum were doing to undermine and isolate Southern Sudan. In that way, friendship between Egypt and the SPLM accorded a status comparable to that which was accorded to sovereign states.

Early 1984 the last summit was held in Aswan between President Hosni Mubarak of Egypt and President Jaafar Nimeiri. One of the topics raised by Nimeiri was "improving the situation in the South", for which he requested military assistance "to clear the remnants of the SPLA". That request achieved nothing. Two days before that summit, we had briefed the Egyptians about the worsening situation in Southern Sudan and how Khartoum was losing ground and how the Government of Sudan was spending about 1.5 million US dollars daily on the war he was not winning. During that exchange with our Egyptian counterparts, we revealed to them that the SPLA fighters had captured Egyptian-made Kalashnikov rifles from the renegade Anya Nya II, who were Khartoum proxies.

As President Mubarak was reliably briefed, he told President Nimeiri that they knew what was going on in Southern Sudan and whatever Nimeiri asked for was turned down, beside Nimeiri's sharp U-turn after the adoption of Sharia laws in Sudan. We told the Egyptians to follow news of the movement through Radio SPLA and that Garang was struggling for a united secular Sudan like Egypt, based on justice and equality and that the doors of the movement were opened to all the Sudanese, who were moving in large numbers to join Garang.

Garang tried his best to reach the Arab countries and succeeded to mend relations with weighty countries in the Arab world, which were supportive to all the regimes in the Sudan, except Iraq, Syria, Yemen, Morocco and the Palestinians for obvious reasons. Each of the four countries had similar problems of racial and religious dimension: Arabism and different Islamic militant brand of Islam as was in Sudan. Almost all the Arab countries deliberately refused to understand the distinct historical reality of the Sudan and so decided to support Arab domination of Sudan, as a gift of Allah to the Arab world, given the availability of its huge oil resource, which could be used to disturb some of the neighbouring African countries. Garang's intention was to block the source of weapons and money that were pouring to Khartoum, and he succeeded to largely reduce to a minimum the flow of weapons and money to the Government of Sudan.

The SPLM was welcomed in most of the Arab countries led by Libya, South Yemen, Egypt, Kuwait, Algeria, Saudi Arabia and the Gulf states except for Bahrain. In Addis Ababa in 1988 Garang met Amr Moussa, the Egyptian Foreign Minister, before he could meet

President Mubarak. That meeting was vital, and it came out very successfully, opening the gate to the Arab world literally. In that meeting Amr Moussa was convinced that the SPLM had a genuine case against successive governments in Sudan since the country had become independent in 1956. After that encounter, a meeting was arranged between Garang and President Hosni Mubarak in which Egyptian military support to Khartoum was stopped and diplomatic relations with the SPLM were established.

When Iraq invaded Kuwait and threatened to advance on Saudi Arabia in 1988, the SPLM under the leadership of Garang, sent solidarity messages to the Amir of Kuwait, Sheikh Sabah Jabir Al Sabah and to King Fahad bin Abdel Aziz Al Saud of Saudi Arabia. In Addis Ababa, Garang sent a two-man delegation to the Saudi Arabia embassy, Dhol Achuil and me, with a strong message conveying the readiness of the movement to dispatch a battalion to participate in the liberation of Kuwait and the defence of the Kingdom of Saudi Arabia.

That stand was essentially based on the principal of international solidarity with all the countries that moved to remove Iraq from Kuwait and defend Saudi Arabia. By standing in support of the friendly State of Kuwait when the Government of Sudan supported the Iraqi aggression, SPLM/A decided to join the world against Iraq, which was intensively fighting us, assisting the Sudan government with arms, tanks, planes, pilots, experts and enormous funds. However, that move served the SPLM/A diplomatically and militarily. It opened impossible avenues to the Arab world.

Our relations continued to develop regularly until President Mubarak met Garang for the first time in June 1988 in Addis Ababa in the corridors of the Organisation of African Unity (OAU) summit, where Garang thanked President Mubarak for granting Southern Sudanese scholarships in Egyptian institutions of higher learning more than twice the intake of what the Sudan was granting to Southern Sudanese.

That fact greatly took President Mubarak by surprise, and he immediately directed his Ministry of High Education to admit Southern Sudanese free and take whoever would apply to study in Egypt. In that year Egypt agreed to allow the SPLM/A to have a representative in Cairo under the Presidency. The first SPLM's representative there was Michael Majok Ayom. He was later succeeded by Daniel Kodi, Arop Moyak, then followed by Ali Kushayb.

Garang made two important visits to Cairo. In his first trip he visited the pyramids and acquainted himself with the history of Egypt and its relations to the Sudan right from antiquity and he visited the tomb of Ali Abdel Latif, one of the Sudanese leading martyrs. He was highly honoured to stage a huge political rally to the Sudanese community in Cairo International Conference Centre and met all the people he wanted to, from President Mubarak downwards. He also met Mohamed Hassanein Heikal and his friend Dr Milad Hanna. Relations with Egypt developed warmly under President Mubarak. And he personally attended the funeral for Garang in Juba. President Mubarak dispatched Consular Khalid Abdel Rahim to Juba to further develop relations before Southern Sudan became an independent country until this very day.

All the eyes of the world were focused on Ethiopia of Mengistu Haile Mariam and eastern parts of the Horn of Africa. In our first days we were incubating in Ethiopia for some time. John Garang was lucky to have begun swimming in a moderate diplomatic climate. For example, Ambassador Bethwell Kiplagat was the person who directed relations between the movement and the government and the people of Kenya, and worked hard to explain our case to the western world. He had excellent relations with the progressive African countries and the democratic world. His office in the Ministry of Foreign Affairs in Nairobi was open daily for our representatives. Opening the route between Southern Sudan and Kenya, Kiplagat built mutual relations since 1972. He was the person who established Sudan Council of

Churches office in Khartoum, as its first general secretary. Through his efforts, assisted by the UN, he paved the road from Kitale to Lokichoggio in 1986 in northwestern Kenya. Ambassador Bethwell Kiplagat was one of the greatest friends of Garang and the people of Southern Sudan.

Garang founded our strong relations with Kenya based on his good knowledge of Kenya since the time of Mau Mau, before it became independent. Kenya was the second country in which he had been, during the early 1960s and he taught in Nyeri. In 1987 Garang visited Kenya, invited by President Daniel arap Moi as organised by Kiplagat. After almost 33 years, Garang came to be attracted by the realities of the struggle, following changes that took place in Ethiopia four years later, and the expansion of the movement to all the borders with neighbours and the peoples' frantic movements, seeking safety.

Garang strongly desired to anchor our presence in a hospitable country with free international access and humanitarian assistance to our people. And as a matter of fact, no country can surpass Kenya in terms of ability to serve Southern Sudan, in which the people have several ethnic relations. The Kenyan-Southern Sudan relations today are based on what our people planted and diversely grew, going back to the days Southern Sudanese were in Kenya as refugees from the 1960s to early 1970s and the opening of the Lokichoggio trade route to Southern Sudan.

To face those who had been deceived by the Arab world, the rest of the world, Garang made it clear that, "Our people did not take the guns as a subset to any foreign power, big or small." He then invited them to visit Southern Sudan to verify his claim. He further said that nobody had pushed the Southern Sudanese to take up arms against the injustice imposed on them.

The desire by the people of Southern Sudan to rid themselves of oppression was realised by the signing of CPA in February 2005, a deal that was crowned by the achievement of statehood in July 2011.

The second fact, which moved the world conscience, was the devastating humanitarian conditions, imposed by the Khartoum government on our people. By exploiting the ecological causes, which caused major drought in 1988 and the subsequent famine, which further devastated the lives of our people in 1998, food international humanitarian organisations were blocked from reaching the needy persons by Khartoum. That apathetic situation convinced most of the civilised world to rush their assistance to the war-effected civilians in the war zones, beginning from 1988 after the launch of the UN sponsored Operation Lifeline Sudan or OLS.

****

From July through to August 1998, following the split within the SPLM/A in 1991, except for the NPA, relations soured between the SPLM/A and the international NGO community. That was the worst year in which famine changed all the equations between humanitarian organisations led by United Nations International Children Educational Fund (UNICEF) and World Food Programme (WFP) on the one hand, and SPLM/SRRA on the other. A high-level committee to evaluate the humanitarian intervention was formed and its chairmanship was assigned to the SPLM to report to the UN upper echelons, the leader of the SPLM, Garang and to the patron of the SRRA, Cdr Salva Kiir. That new status conferred deference on the SPLM/A in the diplomatic and humanitarian communities worldwide. It opened new prosperous doors to move freely internationally. It was an endeavour in which personalities such as Luka Biong and Philip Aguer of SRRA played a major role that cemented cordial relations between SPLM and the humanitarian and diplomatic communities.

The third fact was the dispersal of our people on a large scale around the world, where untold harsh conditions faced them while the war lasted. As if that was not hard enough for the people to bear, internal bloody feuds, which erupted among the people, compelled them to seek safety outside their native homes. Although there was safety in refugee camps, lives of the displaced persons were not rosy. Those were trying for our people wherever they lived, whether at home; in the camps for the displaced persons; refugee camps in neighbouring countries or further afield in the rest of the world where they had migrated to.

The fourth reason, which attracted the international community to stand with us, was our ability to stand firm against the totalitarian Islamist regime in Khartoum.

The fifth reason was our determination to hold our ground and fight on despite the odds; a determination that finally led to victory and for which the peace-loving world respects us.

Our foreign relations were essentially based on the clarity of our case personified in the vision of the movement, and in the way Garang presented it to the world. We were an oppressed people who sought support from friends and peace-loving countries and organisations to achieve our objectives. The movement's policy was centred on introducing our people to others worldwide, to be known and to educate them about the tragedy the people were going through, poor as they were and how to resolve that problem. The cause captured the hearts and minds of the humanitarian world more than in any other time before. This was because of the clarity in which the case was articulated. The NGO community, especially in the US and Western Europe, listened and acted on our appeal for humanitarian support. The world took us from that angle.

It is unfortunate to reveal that from 2005, we appear to have forgotten our friends, mainly organisations, countries and individuals who stood with us during the hour of need. We have failed to recognise those who lent a helping hand, whether diplomatic, humanitarian or even military support, to us during those trying times. Surprisingly enough, we have opened all our doors to swindlers, who have a role in teaching our compatriots how to loot our national resources. Affected by an empty arrogance, we have turned our backs on our true friends and instead befriended countries and individuals, shopping as far as the Gulf States, some of whom collaborated with Khartoum during the war. Such acts are being done under the claim that we are a land-locked and backward country.

Contrary to what Garang had told us to the effect that we should learn how to walk before we can fly, we have ignored that advice. That is the reason we are currently without direction, not knowing who our true friends are, or what to do with our abundant natural resources waiting to be developed and utilised for our own good and for the future generations.

In the remote jungles, bushes and marshes of our vast land in which we were for about twenty-two years, not a mountain of money can ever be compared to the dedication of humanitarian organisations such as the NPA, followed by the World Vision and the World Food Programme (WFP) and people like Dan Eiffe, Kevin Ashley, John Frances, Gordon Wagner, Egil Hagen, Helge Rohn, Adele Sowinska and Hilda Johnson.

Our relations with Norway were firm, cemented by Norwegian People's Aid (NPA). They began not only as a humanitarian agency, but began to render humanitarian support to a people being "oppressed and deprived" and made their point crystal clear to whoever tried to put some political and diplomatic obstacles in their way. Therefore, the NPA, led by steadfast gentlemen such as Helge Rohn, Dan Eiffe and Ken Miller, stood firm with our people. Had it not been for the support rendered by the NPA, the time when NGOs abandoned our areas from 1992 to 1998, no person could imagine where our people would be today.

Besides our comrades in the field, who heroically dug themselves into the trenches at Jebelein on Nimule Road, no person would remember those contributions which were rendered by Dan Eiffe, nicknamed Dan de Mabior, throughout our liberated areas and the NPA under volleys of fire while serving people from bunkers, besides those commanders: Kuol Manyang, Oyay Deng, James Kong and other comrades in arms in defensive positions along Aswa River. It was an impossible time in which we were on the verge of losing a strategic ally, but today, we seem to have forgotten them all, and the inevitable question is: why?

Between Norway and the SPLM/A there was a friendship between the Norwegian Church Aid and the people of Torit and Kapoeta that existed even before the outbreak of the second civil war in 1983. From the mid-1970s, the NCA established a visible permanent presence in Hilieu village en route to Katire on the foot of Imatong Mountain, as its headquarters. The NGO had another post north of Kapoeta known simply as Norwegian. The NCA built a school for the children of the personnel. The kids were being taught subjects based on the Norwegian curriculum at Hilieu. After the war broke out and people heard that Uncle Joseph Oduho, one of the senior leaders of the struggle of the people of Southern Sudan since 1950s, had joined the rebellion, the Norwegians knew that the conflict was destined to spread to Eastern Equatoria. Fearing that eventuality, the NCA decided to pull out of Eastern Equatoria from 1985 to early 1986, ending their presence in Southern Sudan.

In 1986 Malath Joseph Lueth, Damos Deng Ruai and Dhol Achuil, who were in Nairobi, Kenya, were planning to establish a humanitarian wing for the movement, the Sudan Relief and Rehabilitation Association (SRRA). They sought advice and help from the NPA– the Norwegian People's Aid. The time when the three approached the NPA coincided with the arrival of the SPLA forces in Kapoeta area, where they established a firm based in Narus, since 1986 and began to close in on Kapoeta town. Many civilians around Kapoeta deserted and went to areas controlled by the movement. There was no food for the SPLA. Egil Hagen of the NPA was contacted in Nairobi and responded positively. He paid a visit to the area and started to deliver and distribute food to civilians at Narus.

Abdi Hassan, a daring Kenyan-Somali contractor from Kitale took the first trucks, which arrived at Narus from Lokichoggio while dodging mines along the unpaved road. The arrival of Norwegian People's Aid (NPA) marked a dawn of cooperation between the NPA and the SRRA, which extended to the SPLM and the People's Party of Norway from 1987 up to the time the peace agreement was signed in Nairobi in 2005. The NPA supported our people although several Western humanitarian NGOs protested as they claimed the SPLA was interfering with their humanitarian work. For their part, the NPA continued supplying food to every person in need in the areas in Eastern Equatoria where the SPLA forces were operating.

The SPLM/A through OSIL (Operation Save Innocent Lives, a demining non-profit organisation) was among the first fore founders of Non-State Actors Convention on Demining in Geneva, 2002, where Cdr Aleu Ayieny Aleu and I interacted freely with a host of liberation movements well known to states worldwide as armed opposition groups. During the opening of that international gathering, chaired by Mrs Elizabeth Decry, the President of Geneva Parliament, and myself representing the SPLM/A, the representative of Irish Republican Army (IRA) was to my left, while the representative of Moro Islamic Front (MIF) of the Philippines was sitting immediately to my right, facing the representatives of PKK of Kurdistan in Turkey, Polisario from Maghrib, Tamil Tigers from Sri Lanka and other movements. The conference was held at the UN International Hall. That conference gave the SPLM/A deserved recognition, as one of the best performing anti-demining bodies from which humanity could benefit.

That fact convinced the chairperson of the World Non-States

Demining to pay a visit to our areas in 2003, where she was received by John Garang, Riek Machar and more than fifty senior SPLA officers at New Site for what OSIL did. Garang was pleased to have the President of Geneva Parliament at New Site. It was an honour. He was concerned about what should happen to people when peace comes, in a situation in which mines were not cleared from the countryside, where most people abide, especially children, since the government army turned most of the schools into barracks surrounded by mines to defend their positions. OSIL, directed by Aleu Ayieny Aleu, supported by the Norwegian People's Aid (NPA) and other demining agencies, did their best to clear Southern Sudan, Blue Nile and the Nuba Mountains from the deadly dangers of landmines.

33

In Search of a Fitting Epitaph

Just as he was gracefully ushered into leadership in a helicopter in 1983, John Garang was sadly taken from the leadership in a helicopter crash on July 30, 2005. Garang departed with only what was on him. No home, no bank account and no hatred. People may differ about his legendary life. There were those pushed by envy to hate the man for what he might not have done and refused to forgive him. Forgetting it was his commitment, bravery, dedication and humility, which were the main attributes that lifted him to surmount those mountainous military and political hurdles with utmost ease.

There were hard times though, which the man passed with no adequate answers. Like the stories about how comrades in the struggle: Lokurnyang, Martin Majier Gai, Malath Joseph Lueth, Makur Aleiyou, Joseph Oduho and others kept hanging, requiring answers from those who were nearer to where they lost their lives, to remain as the saddest spots in the history of the movement and of Garang as the leader. Although he might have been far from committing them, the fact that no steps were seen taken against those who committed them remains a stigma. Those are sad stories people attempted to stick at random on individuals of whom Garang was one. All the stories above could metaphorically be described as the tip of the iceberg about Garang, the man. One believes many people have stories. By sending my call to those who knew the man, I am looking for a better way to collect his experiences to benefit our people. Indeed, John Garang was a gift to his nation.

When Garang produced his Bible, the time we had fellowship in the residence of General Elly Tumwine in Kampala in 1998, Christian Military Fellowship, I was surprised to know that Dr Garang could be described as a practising Christian in his own way. He consulted his Bible privately and regularly for spiritual revitalisation and wisdom. That was why he quoted and referred to the Bible on different occasions. But he was not that showy with his spirituality. That was the reason why what some people perceived to be prophecy whenever some of his predictions turned out to be real, his buffalo's calculated charge, his humility, his tiger tactical moves, his inspiring intellectual acumen, his love for his people, his cutting wit, his amazing gentility, his warm heart, his entertaining smiles, his infectious laughter, his capturing wisdom and his dedication to the land, exulted him a great leader. With that legion of attributes, Dr John Garang de Mabior Atem departed leaving us a legend of a man who diligently and bravely led his life with humility, honesty, honour and pride.

Acronyms and Abbreviations

A/Cdr: Alternate Commander was the SPLA rank for officers from Major to Commander, which in turn comprised all conventional ranks from Major to General.

BCE: Before Current Era, (previously BC or Before Christ)

CE: Current Era, previously Anno Domini (AD) or the Year of Our Lord

Cde: Shortened form of comrade, more generally, comrade in arms. This was commonly used by SPLM/A when colleagues addressed each other, especially during the war (1983-2005). After the war, the usage has declined although more senior members of the SPLM or those in the military prefer to use the word.

Cdr: Abbreviation of commander

EPLF: Eritrean People's Liberation Front was the secessionist movement from the former Eritrean province, which was fighting for the secession for statehood, which it achieved in early 1990s.

IRA: Irish Republican Army

NAM: National Action Movement, an underground organisation formed at the time some members of the Southern intelligentsia were showing reservations about the Addis Ababa Agreement, power struggle among politicians in the autonomous region, which the ruling Northern class was exploiting for their own benefit.

POLISARO/Polisaro: the organisation that was championing for the independence of the Spanish Sahara from Morocco

NPA: Norwegian People's Aid

NIF: National Islamic Front was the political organisation that campaigned for an Islamic constitution for Sudan. It was led by Dr Hassan Abdallah el Turabi, a former law lecturer at the University of Khartoum in the early 1960s. After the overthrow in 1964 of the military dictatorship headed by General Ibrahim Abboud, Turabi established Islamic Charter Front. Years later, the name was changed to National Congress Party under the regime of General Omar Bashir.

DUP: Democratic Unionist Party

NAM: Nation Action Movement

NAMLA: National Action Movement and Liberation Army

NDA: National Democratic Alliance

NCP: National Congress Party

OSIL: Operation Save Innocent Lives, a demining organisation created and run by SPLM/A, headed by Aleu Ayieny Aleu, an SPLA officer after he was wounded and then demobilised afterwards as the founding director.

Payam: The first tier below the county as an administrative unit in South Sudan

USAP: Union of African Parties

SAC: Sudan African Congress

SSU: Sudan Socialist Union

Uncle: In the context of South Sudan, when a person addresses another person as an uncle, in most cases there is no blood relationship between the two. The word is used as a form of honorific, especially for someone who is an elder.

SPLM/SPLA: Sudan People's Liberation Movement/Sudan People's Army, the political and military components of the organisations that were waging war against the Government of Sudan from

1983- 2005. For convenience, it is usually written as SPLM/A.

Colonel Mengistu Haile Mariam: The full name of the former Ethiopian leader is Mengistu Haile Mariam. Ethiopian naming system takes the first name, in this case, Mengistu in the place of surname. In this case it is Colonel or President Mengistu, not Colonel or President Haile Mariam (Haile Mariam is taken as one, not two separate names). Mengistu, who held the rank of lieutenant colonel was often referred to by the Western media as Colonel Mengistu Haile Mariam. After the transition from the Dergue, the ruling military council, Mengistu became head of the Workers Party of Ethiopia in July 1984, after which he had to be addressed as President Mengistu Haile Mariam, or simply President Mengistu.

The Sudan/Sudan: the word is a translation of Arabic "*es sudan*", literally meaning "the black". The English equivalent was translated into "the Soudan/Sudan". It has been a long time since the definite article "the" was dropped. Now we have the plain Sudan instead of the Sudan.

Index

Ababa 41, 142, 191, 203
Abbas 45, 47-9, 112
Abboud 102, 216
Abdalla 35, 39, 58, 90-1, 103-4, 146
Abdel 31, 50, 53, 75, 79, 91, 95, 103-5, 145, 157-8, 160, 177, 191, 201, 203-4
Abdi 210
Abel 103, 177
Abere 43
Aborom 18, 85
Abugor 48, 51, 65, 89
Abuja 130-132, 161
Abul 29-30
Abur 57
Abyei 12, 14, 16, 18, 20, 22, 24, 26-8, 30, 33-4, 36, 38, 40, 42, 44, 48, 50, 52, 54, 56-8, 60, 62, 64, 66, 70, 72, 74, 76, 78, 80, 82, 84, 88, 90, 92, 94, 96, 98, 100, 102, 104, 106, 110, 112, 114, 116, 118, 120, 122, 124, 126, 130, 132, 134, 136, 138, 140, 144, 146, 150, 154, 156, 158, 160, 162, 164, 166, 170, 172, 174, 176, 180, 182, 188, 190, 192, 194, 196, 200, 202, 204, 206, 208, 210, 212, 216
Achiek 38-39, 48, 89
Achol 53
Achuek 15
Achuil 203, 209
Adam 50, 53, 104, 145, 157-8, 177, 191
Addis 41, 53, 55, 111, 142, 191, 203
Addis Ababa 22-23, 41-4, 51, 53-4, 57, 63, 75, 79, 99, 111-2, 114, 123, 136-8, 142, 155, 177, 191, 202-3, 215
Adele 208

Adwok 103
Adyang 103
Afaf 104
Aff 21, 113, 147, 156, 201, 204, 208
Afhad 31
Africa 15, 72, 79, 99, 109, 112, 116, 123, 135, 146, 150, 176, 199-200, 204
African 15, 21-2, 45, 79, 88, 90, 99, 103, 111-3, 135-6, 139, 145-6, 160, 176, 197, 202-4, 216
Africanists 146
Afwerki 135
Agar 167, 173, 175
Ager 103
Aggrey 103
Agha 82
Agostino 21
Aguer 206
Aguet 57
Ahmed 74-75, 91, 104, 155, 184, 201
Ajab 104
Ajak 11, 137, 166, 174
Ajang 16, 166, 173-4
Ajawin 65, 83, 89
Ajok 47
Akasha 103
Akobo 35-36, 56-7
Akoi 18
Akok 33, 58
Akol 38, 40-1, 43, 49-50, 65, 71, 82-3, 89-90, 103, 191, 200
Akon 163
Akoon 154
Akot 35, 175
Akuol 18
Akuot 22, 58, 63
Alas 10
Albright 135
Aleiyou 212
Aleu 152, 210-1, 216
Alfred 22, 30, 111
Algeria 202
Alhaj 11
Ali 31, 79, 82, 102-4, 141, 145, 147, 155-7, 197, 204
Alier 103
Aligo 11, 17
Alikaya 11, 17
Allah 126, 202
Alor 11, 16, 112, 130-2, 160, 173, 198, 200
Aluong 16, 166
Amarat 40
America 23, 34, 109, 138, 200
American 39, 135-6, 138, 144, 200
Americans 137
Amilcar 21
Amin 103, 146, 155
Amir 203

Amon 33, 38, 111
Amr 135, 202-3
Amum 16, 35
Anai 33, 38
Anakdiar 83
Andrea 22
Andrew 135
Angela 135
Angelo 24, 89
Angolan 135
Angolans 41
Angudri 141
Annan 135
Anne 27
Anno 215
Anta 79, 185
Anwar 103
Anya 22-23, 28-9, 34, 36-7, 44, 52, 57, 68-9, 88, 97-9, 111-2, 141, 155, 165, 175, 193, 202
Anyar 166
Anyieth 65
Apieu 166
Arab 36, 44, 73, 91, 93, 103, 109, 126, 142, 147, 177, 200, 202-3, 205
Arab domination 202
Arabia 202-203
Arabic 15, 24-5, 42, 64, 113, 148, 180, 192, 217
Arabism 92-93, 106, 114, 202
Arabs 93, 126

Araki 103
Arap 113
Areng 18
Ariath 52, 57
Arman 16, 104, 106
Arok 38-43, 52
Arol 80
Arop 55, 173, 204
Aru 27
Arua 146
Aruei 18, 20
Ashley 208
Askari 103
Asmara 80, 107, 123, 156
Assosa 70
Aswa 209
Aswad 173
Aswan 201
Ata 104
Atabani 106
Atari 89
Atem 9-11, 15-6, 18-23, 27, 29, 31, 33, 35, 39, 41, 43, 45, 47, 49, 51-3, 57-9, 63, 65, 67, 69, 71, 75, 77, 79, 83, 85, 87, 89, 91, 93, 97, 99, 101, 103, 105, 107, 109, 111, 113, 117, 121, 123, 125, 127, 129, 131, 135-7, 139, 141, 143, 145, 147, 149, 151, 153, 155, 157, 159, 161, 165, 167, 169, 171, 173, 175, 177, 179, 183, 185, 187, 189,

191, 195-7, 199, 201, 203, 205, 207, 209, 213, 215
Athithi 20
Atlanta 136
Atlantic 200
Atong 197
Aunt 82
Aweil 37
Awet 34-35, 175
Awulian 18
Awuol 38, 89
Axis 69
Ayieny 152, 210-1, 216
Ayod 36-37, 59, 85-6, 166
Ayom 204
Ayong 52
Ayuak 39, 50
Ayuel 83
Ayuen 21
Azande 175, 201
Aziz 50, 53, 91, 95, 157-8, 177, 191, 203
Baba 112
Babangida 135
Badri 31, 103, 136
Baghir 104
Bahr 20, 33, 36, 40, 58-9, 110, 162, 166, 175, 190
Bahrain 202
Bakheit 103
Bambuti 176
Banna 35-36

Bany 52, 111, 191, 197
Bari 22
Baroness 135
Bashir 16, 95, 100, 124, 126, 145-8, 155, 158, 160-1, 216
Battalion 33, 38
Baz 135
Bazara 83
Bazigino 174
Bazingau 174
Bazingwe 174
Bazzuga 145
Beja 92, 94
Bemba 145-146
Benghazi 130, 147-8
Benjamin 29-30, 33-4, 38, 50, 58, 103
Benning 33, 136
Benson 47
Bentiu 37, 57, 84, 97, 157
Bernard 135
Bethuel 113, 136
Bethwell 204-205
Biar 169, 173-4
Bidiet 98, 112
Bil 50
Bilal 155
Bilpam 44, 154, 192
Bineya 104
Biong 53, 169, 206
Bior 16, 82-3, 174
Bismarck 26

Blue 37, 52, 69, 87, 92, 102, 120, 124, 165, 178, 183, 193, 211
Bol 26-27, 33, 35, 39, 47, 58, 137, 197
Bolaad 103, 177
Bolsheviks 26
Boma 31, 35, 58, 182
Bona 55, 98, 131, 139
Bonga 118, 154, 189
Bor 18, 21, 29-30, 33, 35-6, 38-41, 46, 53, 56-9, 62-3, 84, 166
Bou 153, 174
Branson 135
Brian 16, 136
British 84, 110, 135, 139
Brooking 151
Bullen 103
Bunning 79
Bussere 20, 29-30
Buth 103
Cabral 21
Cairo 80, 204
Callery 16
Caribbean 146
Carter 135-136
Castro 135, 200
Cdr 11-12, 45, 71, 82-4, 86, 105-6, 111-2, 130, 152, 154-5, 157-9, 163-4, 166-7, 169, 172, 175-7, 187, 189-193, 197, 206, 210
Cdrs 167
Central Equatoria 22
Certifi 26
Chaat 56-57
Chad 136, 199
Charles 38
Cheikh 79, 185
Chevron 109
Chiengkuach 16
Children 206
Chok 84
Chol 19, 34, 38-9, 50, 196
Christian 24, 99, 213
Christianity 15, 93
Chuang 16, 83, 159, 166, 182
Chukudum 94, 105
Chuol 35, 58
Cirillo 12
Cirino 11
Clement 12, 103
Congo 136, 140-1, 145-6, 154, 171, 173, 175
Congolese 140-141
Congressman 135-138
Congressmen 138
Coordination 40
Costa 58
Cox 135
Cuba 191, 199-200
Cuban 135, 200
Cubans 200

Cush 185
Cushitic 25
Dafallah 90-91
Dahab 89, 91
Dak 35
Dam 94
Damazin 83
Damos 209
Dan 16, 136, 208-9
Daniel 24, 31, 34-5, 59, 89, 98, 113, 135, 141, 175, 204-5
Daoud 103, 177
Dar 21
Darfur 52, 87, 92, 95, 124, 157-8, 176-7
Darfuris 92
Dau 16, 136-7, 173
David 98, 112
Davies 135
Dawood 177
Dawson 21, 78
Deby 136
Decry 210
Defi 129
Demining 210-211
Denay 136
Deng 11, 14-8, 31, 38, 52-3, 59, 80, 83-4, 88-9, 97, 102-3, 112, 130-2, 136-7, 160, 166-7, 169, 173-7, 182, 187, 198, 200, 209
Dennis 136
Dergue 217

Dhol 203, 209
Diabio 166
Dick 117
Dieu 84
Diing 111-112
Dima 72
Din 104
Dinka 36, 53, 201
Diop 79, 185
Disciplinary 44, 81
Diu 103
Domini 215
Donald 135
Donato 53
Dreyfus 30
Duk 85
Duku 171
Dungu 140
Duot 16, 166
Dut 27
Dutch 75
Early 130-131, 146, 153, 201
East 18, 85, 94, 123
Eastern 64, 73, 105, 120, 124, 196, 200
Eastern Equatoria 150, 209-210
Economic 149
Edin 91, 106
Eduardo 21, 135
Edward 12, 14, 16, 18, 20, 22, 24, 26, 28, 30, 33-4, 36, 38, 40, 42, 44, 48, 50, 52, 54, 56, 58,

60, 62, 64, 66, 70, 72, 74, 76, 78, 80, 82, 84, 88-90, 92, 94, 96, 98, 100, 102, 104, 106, 110, 112, 114, 116, 118, 120, 122, 124, 126, 130, 132, 134, 136, 138, 140, 144, 146, 150, 154, 156, 158, 160, 162, 164, 166, 170, 172, 174-6, 180, 182, 188, 190, 192, 194, 196, 200, 202, 204, 206, 208, 210, 212, 216
Egil 208, 210
Egypt 79, 123, 165, 199, 201-2, 204
Egyptian 100, 106, 135-6, 185, 201-3
Egyptians 199, 201-2
Eiff 16, 136, 208-9
Eissa 103
Eliaba 112-113
Elizabeth 210
Elly 213
Emad 201
Emmanuel 57
English 26, 148, 180, 192, 217
Epitaph 9, 212
Equatoria 57, 105, 110, 142, 146, 169, 193
Equatoria Region 169
Eretria 135
Erkawit 55
Europe 26, 73, 114, 137, 207
European 158

Everybody 28
Ezo 175
Ezzo 174
Faculty 33, 38, 41, 53, 78
Fadhul 91
Fadl 155
Fadlallah 74-75, 184
Fahad 203
Farouq 103-104, 135
Fasher 157-158
Fathi 104
Fatima 104
Faustino 103
Fazel 103
Ferdinand 103
Fidel 135, 200
Fiji 145
Frances 208
Francis 14, 33, 136, 155
French 30, 135
Fur 157-158, 160
Gaboush 45, 47-50, 103, 112
Gaddafi 135, 147-8, 160
Gahoth 60
Gai 58, 63, 84, 212
Gak 18, 84-5, 196
Gambela 43-44, 63, 84, 98, 159
Gangthi 85
Garang 9-37, 39-41, 43-5, 47, 49, 51-7, 59, 62-89, 91-114, 116-167, 169-179, 181-209, 211-3, 215

Gasim 29-31, 103
Gassim 136
Gatluak 83
Gbadolite 145-146
Gbuatala 102-103, 141-2
Gbuatalas 107
Geneva 210-211
George 29-31, 34, 38-9, 50
Georgia 79, 136
Gergis 104
Germany 26, 199
Getachew 43
Ghanaian 135-136
Ghazal 20, 36, 40, 59, 110, 162, 166, 175, 190
Gier 16, 83, 159-160, 166, 182
Gihon 112, 185
God 10, 76, 104, 126
Gordon 38, 48, 82-4, 89, 97, 103, 176, 208
Grinnell 21-23, 78-9
Guiny 39
Gulf 202, 208
Gulu 146
Gum 103
Gumwel 80
Hagen 208, 210
Hague 75
Haile 41, 43, 54-5, 63, 116, 135, 143-4, 155-6, 192, 200, 204, 217
Haj 155, 163

Hajj 104
Hamish 64
Hanna 136, 204
Hardolu 91-92
Harry 117
Hashim 104
Hassan 40-43, 55, 104, 113, 146, 210, 216
Hassanein 135, 204
Heikal 135, 204
Helen 53
Helge 208
Henry 102, 154
Heyala 167, 191
High Command 196
Hilal 34, 50
Hilary 103
Hilda 15, 135, 208
Hilieu 191, 196, 209
Hilu 50, 53, 157-8, 177, 191
Hino 83
Hiteng 11
Hosni 100, 135, 201, 203
Hoth 16, 82-3, 97, 166-7, 169, 172-3, 175-6, 182
Humility 129
Hussein 136
Ibba 171, 173-5
Ibrahim 29-30, 102, 104, 135, 216
Idi 146
Idriss 136

Ikk 25
Ikotos 167
Illiteracy 194
Imatong 209
Incursion 169
Ingessana 92
Instantly 100
Intibaha 74, 100
Intisar 104
Iowa 29, 33, 78, 137
Iraq 202-203
Iraqi 203
Irish 210, 215
Isaac 83
Isaiah 70, 174
Isaias 135
Ishaq 74-75, 184
Isiro 140-141
Islam 15, 92-3
Islamising 113
Islamist 74, 90, 177, 207
Ismail 40-43, 48, 50, 55
Isoke 150
Italy 199
Itang 43-44, 63, 72-3, 83-4, 97, 154, 160, 191
Jaafar 30, 89-90, 104, 109-110, 193, 201
Jabir 203
Jadein 201
Jaden 103
Jalal 104
Jallab 48, 50
Jamaa 103
Jambo 160
James 16, 65, 82-3, 97, 112-3, 135, 166, 169, 172-3, 175-6, 182, 192, 209
Jaramogi 22
Jazouli 90-91, 104
Jebel 82, 158
Jebelein 208
Jekou 154-155, 165, 167
Jerry 135
Jesus 140
Jet 146
Jewish 30
Jibril 28-29
Jimmy 135-136
Joesph 54
John 9-16, 18-9, 21-3, 25-31, 33-7, 39-41, 43, 45, 47, 49, 51-7, 59, 63-5, 67-9, 71-2, 74-9, 81, 83, 85, 87-9, 91, 93, 97-9, 101, 103, 105-7, 109-111, 113, 117-121, 123-5, 127, 129, 131-2, 134-7, 139, 141-3, 145-9, 151, 153-5, 157-9, 161, 165, 167, 169, 171-3, 175, 177, 179, 182-3, 185, 187, 189, 191, 193, 195-9, 201, 203-5, 207-9, 211-3, 215
Johnson 15, 135, 208
Jonglei 18-19, 59, 150

Joseph 22-23, 27, 29-30, 54-5, 99, 103, 111, 135, 142, 209, 212
Juba 11-12, 33, 35-6, 39, 56-9, 68, 70-2, 77-8, 100-1, 122, 161, 164, 189-190, 193, 204
Jukuriya 111
Julius 29, 135
Jumi 141
Jumma 85, 104, 146
Jur 162
Justin 54-55, 200
Justus 113
Juuk 11
Kabashi 11, 50, 103
Kabila 135, 146
Kachu 173
Kadugli 52
Kagame 135
Kahinda 147
Kajbar 94
Kajo 70-72, 88, 166, 174
Kalashnikov 202
Kamal 104, 155
Kameir 14, 79, 103
Kamlin 92
Kampala 10, 22, 112, 124, 196, 213
Kapoeta 37, 57, 88, 166, 209
Karari 50
Karen 98, 113
Kassala 157, 165
Katire 209
Kaunda 22, 113, 135, 138
Kaya 70-72, 88, 146, 166
Keji 70-72, 88, 166, 174
Kelueljang 33
Ken 208
Kenana 110
Kenneth 135, 138
Kenya 10-11, 20-1, 112-3, 187-8, 199, 204-5, 209
Kenyan 11, 98, 135-6
Kerubino 35-37, 39-40, 46, 58, 112, 182, 191, 197
Kevin 208
Khalid 14, 45, 91, 95, 103, 105, 136-7, 139, 204
Khalifa 155
Khaliq 201
Khamis 48, 50
Khartoum 9, 23, 27, 30-1, 33, 35, 38-9, 44-8, 52-7, 59-60, 65, 72-4, 78, 80-2, 88-92, 94-5, 97-9, 105-8, 110-2, 114, 118, 123-4, 126-7, 133, 137, 144, 146, 148, 154-8, 163, 183, 188-9, 191, 199-203, 205-8
Khor 71, 83
Kibaki 11, 135
Kibir 158
Kiir 11-12, 16, 29, 34-5, 62-3, 83, 86, 100, 152, 157-8, 163, 166-7, 187-193, 197-8, 206

Kinshasa 140
Kiplagat 113, 136, 204-5
Kisangani 140
Kitale 205, 210
Koat 98
Kobar 90
Kober 49
Kober Prison 49
Kodi 24, 89, 204
Kodok 83
Kofi 135
Kok 38, 65, 87, 89-90, 107
Kolok 26
Kong 82-84, 97, 154, 198, 209
Kongor 18
Kordofan 92
Koreib 64
Kosti 82
Kou 89
Kouchner 135
Kuany 21, 82-3
Kuanyin 35-37, 39-40, 46, 58, 112, 182, 191, 197
Kuek 35
Kuir 197
Kukudu 169-170, 173
Kumolo 53
Kunijwok 89-90
Kuol 11, 18, 52, 84, 132, 159-160, 167, 173, 198, 209
Kur 47
Kurdistan 210

Kurmuk 70, 72, 83
Kushayb 204
Kuur 21
Kuwa 45, 52-3, 102-3, 105-6, 167
Kuwait 202-203
Kwesi 136
Laat 50
Lado 111
Ladu 22
Lagu 22-23, 29-30, 54-5, 103, 142
Lainya 70-71, 166
Lam 38, 40-1, 43, 49-50, 65, 71, 82-3, 89-90, 191, 200
Lanka 210
Lasu 141
Latif 31, 79, 103, 204
Laurent 135, 146
Lazarus 15
Lecturers 91
Leland 136-138
Lenin 26
Leyland 135
Liberation 34, 44, 53, 56, 59, 63-4, 70, 121, 215-6
Libya 54, 130, 135, 147, 165, 199, 202
Libyan 147, 160
Libyans 160
Lifeline 206
Lino 12, 14, 16, 18, 20, 22, 24,

26, 28, 30, 33-4, 36, 38, 40, 42, 44, 48, 50, 52, 54, 56, 58, 60, 62, 64, 66, 70, 72, 74, 76, 78, 80, 82, 84, 88, 90, 92, 94, 96, 98, 100, 102, 104, 106, 110, 112, 114, 116, 118, 120, 122, 124, 126, 130, 132, 134, 136, 138, 140, 144, 146, 150, 154, 156, 158, 160, 162, 164, 166, 170, 172, 174, 176, 180, 182, 188, 190, 192, 194, 196, 200, 202, 204, 206, 208, 210, 212, 216

Lions 94
Lirongo 166, 175
Loboni 22
Lobonok 22
Logali 103
Lokichoggio 205, 210
Lokurnyang 35, 212
London 58, 138-9
Longkuei 70, 72
Lotuho 125
Louis 145
Loyola 102, 141
Loyolas 107
Lozolia 25
Lual 15, 58, 111-2
Luckily 83, 146, 187
Lueth 21, 27, 209, 212
Luigi 103
Luka 169, 206

Lul 102
Lumumba 88
Lwoki 103
Maathai 135
Maban 136
Mabior 9-11, 13, 15, 18-9, 21, 23, 27-9, 31, 33, 35, 39, 41, 43, 45, 47, 49, 51, 53, 57, 59, 63, 65, 67, 69, 71, 75, 77, 79, 83, 85, 87, 89, 91, 93, 97, 99, 101, 103, 105, 107, 109, 111, 113, 117, 121, 123, 125, 127, 129, 131, 135, 137, 139, 141, 143, 145, 147, 149, 151, 153, 155, 157, 159, 161, 165, 167, 169, 171, 173, 175, 177, 179, 183, 185, 187, 189, 191, 195-7, 199, 201, 203, 205, 207, 209, 213, 215
Mabok 39
Mabur 27
Mach 166, 173, 175
Machar 71, 82-3, 91, 118-9, 192, 200, 211
Machiech 34, 38, 155
Madeleine 135
Madut 55, 131
Magar 38-39, 48-50, 89
Maghrib 210
Magwe 164
Mahdi 51-52, 75, 80, 113, 165
Mahdiyya 87

Mahgoub 23
Mahmoud 103, 201
Mai 16, 97, 166
Maiwut 82
Majak 132, 160
Majid 105
Majier 212
Majok 16, 21, 27, 166, 173, 175, 204
Makashfi 50-51
Makoi 28-29
Makur 212
Malakal 35, 37, 39, 59, 63, 82-3
Malath 27, 209, 212
Malik 167, 173, 175
Malual 16, 18, 27-8, 39-40, 42-3, 50-1, 54-7, 60, 84, 156
Malwal 55, 98, 131, 139
Mama 19, 79
Mamun 104
Mamur 166
Manan 104
Manaseer 92, 94
Mandela 135
Manoah 27
Mansour 14, 45, 103-5, 136-7, 139
Manute 137
Manyang 11, 38, 89, 167, 198, 209
Manyiel 83, 200
Mara 158
Marco 38
Mariam 41, 43, 54-5, 63, 116, 135, 143-4, 155-6, 192, 200, 204, 217
Maridi 141-142, 154, 166, 169, 173, 175
Marko 34
Marshall 91
Mary 135
Mathiang 27-28, 39-40, 42-3, 50-1, 54-5, 80, 155-6
Matthews 98
Mau 205
Mayen 53
Mayom 169, 173-4
Mbeki 135
Mboro 103
Medani 103
Mekelle 144
Mekki 52-53, 103, 105-6
Meles 135
Mengistu 41, 43, 54-5, 63, 116-7, 127, 135, 143-4, 155-6, 192, 200, 204, 217
Mesfi 63
Mete 166
Miakol 52
Michael 204
Michel 135
Mickey 138
Micky 135-136
Microphones 154

Milad 136, 204
Military 33, 46, 90-1, 175, 213
military operations 167
Mior 97, 177
Mirghani 107
Mizan 182
Mobutu 135, 140, 146
Mohamed 54, 103-4, 107, 135, 157, 197, 204
Mohammed 29-30, 82-3, 89-90, 103, 107, 109, 155-6
Moi 98, 113, 135, 205
Mom 89
Mondlane 21
Monyluak 173
Monywiir 173
Moro 210
Morobo 70-72, 146, 166
Morocco 202, 216
Moulana 107
Mousa 104
Moussa 135, 202-3
Moya 193
Moyak 204
Mozambicans 41
Mozambique 135
Muamar 135, 147, 161
Mubarak 100, 135, 201-4
Mulla 173, 175
Mum 89
Mundri 166, 175
Mundukuru 142

Muortat 38, 48, 89, 103
Mupoi 166, 174
Mursi 50
Musa 39, 50, 155
Museveni 22, 112, 124, 130, 135, 147-8
Muslim 44
Muslims 106, 177
Mustafa 53, 82, 103
Muthrif 106
Mwai 11, 135
Mwalimu 135
Naandi 166, 174-5
Nabanga 169, 171-5
Nabiapai 166
Nagero 166
Nagib 136
Nairobi 10-11, 22, 54, 74, 98, 113-4, 120, 132, 141-2, 144, 157, 188, 196, 204, 209-210
Naivasha 74, 98, 129, 152, 156-7, 162, 188, 197
Nakuru 113
Namibia 199
Namibian 135
Namibians 41
Narus 209-210
Nasir 23, 82-3, 91, 97, 166, 182
Natale 145
Natsios 135
Nazareth 43
Nebbi 146

Nelson 135
Neto 21, 88
Ngachigak 35, 102
Ngor 155
Nguesso 136
Ngun 17
Nhial 57, 80, 83, 88-9, 102-3, 187, 200
Nigeria 130
Nigerian 79, 131
Nikanora 38-39, 48-50, 89
Nile 17, 19, 37, 52, 69-70, 79, 83, 87, 92, 98, 102, 120, 124, 146, 150, 165, 178, 183, 185, 193, 201, 211
Nimeiri 23, 30, 39, 41, 45, 73, 89-90, 109-110, 193, 200-2
Nimir 104
Nimule 208
Nixon 137
Northerners 106-107, 122
Norway 199, 208-210
Norwegian 208-211, 216
Norwegians 209
Nuba 25, 37, 48, 52-3, 59, 87, 92, 102, 105, 112, 120, 124, 165, 178-9, 183, 193, 211
Nubawi 105
Nubians 92
Nuer 36, 84, 86, 97, 165
Nujoma 21, 135
Nur 103, 107

Nya 22-23, 28-9, 34-7, 44, 52, 57, 68-9, 88, 97-9, 111-2, 141, 155, 175, 179, 193, 202
Nyachiluk 35, 102
Nyandeng 19, 27, 79, 84, 160
Nyanthon 27
Nyerere 135
Nyeri 21, 205
Nyot 38, 43, 47-8, 53, 87, 89, 107
Nyuak 18
Nyuon 52, 59, 111, 154, 191, 197
Nzara 166, 169, 173-7
Obasanjo 131-132, 135
Obiech 85
Obote 166
Odinga 21, 135
Oduho 99, 111, 209, 212
Offi 40, 139
Oginga 21-22
Ohure 103, 166
Okerruk 166
Okiech 89
Ole 113
Oliver 171
Olusegun 135
Omar 16, 95, 100, 124, 126, 145-8, 155, 158, 160-1, 216
Omdurman 25, 50
Omer 54, 91, 104, 157-8, 160
Omrah 104

Oris 146
Osama 103
Osman 90-91, 103, 107, 156-7, 197
Otafi 147
Othwonh 35
Oyay 11, 16, 83, 136-7, 166-7, 169, 173-6, 182, 198, 209
Pachong 26
Pagak 82, 159
Pageri 197
Pakwach 146
Pal 63
Palestinians 202
Pangs 56
Panyagoor 59
Paterno 89
Paul 102-103, 135, 141, 174
Payam 18
Payne 135
Paysama 31, 103
Penal 81
Peter 34, 38, 43, 47-8, 53, 65, 87, 89-90, 107
Peters 176
Philippines 210
Pibor 35-37, 59, 166
Pieng 16, 167
Pierre 145-146, 166
Pinywudo 72-73, 136
Pochalla 35-37, 59
Polisario 210

Prah 136
Prendergast 136
Presidency 201, 204
Prime Minister 52, 75, 135
Prof 103, 136
Qaddafi 161
Quran 23
Quranic 24
Rafi 166
Rahim 204
Rahman 75, 91, 103-4, 145, 157, 160
Raila 135
Rajab 201
Ramadhan 48, 51, 65, 89, 104
Ramla 71
Ras 169
Rashaida 25, 92, 94
Rawlings 135
Rebecca 19, 79, 84, 160, 196
Rehabilitation 209
Relaxation 182
Renk 47, 82
Renze 174
Renzi 167
Richard 135, 137, 173, 175
Riek 71, 82-3, 91, 118-9, 164, 192, 200, 211
Rimeila 48
Rimenze 174
Roadmap 62
Robinson 135

Rodney 21, 135
Roger 16, 136
Rohn 208
Romani 103
Ronaldo 102, 141
Roro 103
Rostum 82
Rowland 110-111, 135, 139
Ruai 209
Rumbek 20, 26, 37, 157, 166, 187-9, 201
Russia 26
Rwandan 135
Saads 107
Sabah 203
Sadiq 51-52, 75, 80, 113, 165
Sadur 48-49
Saed 106, 155
Saeed 16
Saeid 83, 104, 165
Sahara 216
Sailing 109
Sakure 166, 175
Salaam 21
Salah 106
Salam 103
Salim 165
Salva 11-12, 16, 29, 34-5, 63, 83, 86, 100, 152, 157-8, 163, 166-7, 187, 189-193, 197-8, 206
Salwa 104
Sam 21, 135
Samora 135
Samuel 11, 27, 47, 58, 63, 103, 141, 175
Sanhouri 104
Santos 135
Saturnino 103
Saud 203
Saudi 40, 202-3
Sawiris 136
Scientifi 185
Sebit 175
Secondo 58
Seko 135, 146
Senegalese 185
Sergeant 47, 62
Sese 135, 146
Sharhabiil 104
Sharia 23, 38, 50, 103, 110, 126, 202
Sheijara 39
Sheikh 203
Siddiq 35-36, 106
Simba 162
Sirr 33, 38
Sirte 160-161
Sobat 84, 86, 97, 154, 182
Socialism 22
Soli 52
Somalis 41
Soudan 217
Southern Sudan 21-22, 34, 36-9,

41, 44, 56-8, 60-1, 68, 71-2, 87, 94, 98, 106, 109-110, 113, 121-2, 125-6, 128, 130, 136-7, 143-6, 149-152, 178, 184, 188-9, 191-3, 199-202, 204-5, 209, 211
Southerner 107
Southerners 31, 105
Soviet 73
Sowinska 208
Spanish 216
Sri 210
Stalin 26
Stanislaus 31, 103
Stephen 82-83, 97
Stewardship 69
Sudan 9, 11, 13-6, 18-20, 24-6, 31, 33-5, 37, 39, 41, 44-6, 50-7, 59, 64, 67, 69, 71-3, 78-81, 87-8, 90-5, 97, 99-104, 106-111, 113-4, 117-8, 120-7, 129, 138-141, 143-9, 151, 154, 157-8, 164-5, 169, 177, 179, 183-5, 187, 189, 194, 196, 199-204, 206, 209, 216-7
Sudanese 12-14, 21, 23-4, 30-1, 33-4, 38, 40, 43-4, 46-7, 51-3, 59-60, 68, 70, 78-80, 87, 89, 92-4, 99-100, 102-8, 114-5, 121-2, 124-6, 139, 142, 145-6, 155, 160, 163, 165, 177, 179-180, 202-4
Sudd 19, 150
Sue 174
Sukhun 193
Sumbeiywo 15
Sunday 11, 104, 136
Surur 112-113
Susan 135-136, 160
Suwar 89, 91
Syria 202
Taban 84
Tactician 153
Tafari 182
Taha 50, 103-4, 156, 197
Tahir 82-83
Taj 91
Tambura 174-175
Tamil 210
Tanzania 21-22, 191
Tanzanian 22, 29, 135
Tarbush 104
Tayeb 54
Ted 136
Teus 25
Timmons 33, 78
Tipis 113
Tom 117
Tombura 153, 166, 174-6
Tonj 20, 80, 85, 161-2, 166
Tore 171
Tore Wande 174
Torit 68, 76, 102, 125, 141, 164, 166, 191, 209

Torn 150
Tripoli 148, 161
Trojan 39
Tsore 70, 72
Tumwine 213
Turabi 113, 146, 216
Tut 58, 63, 83
Twic 18, 85
Uduk 25
Uele 169
Uganda 10, 22, 70, 112, 124, 146, 157, 165, 199
Ugandan 12, 135, 146-7
Ulang 82-85
Ulu 169
Umma 80, 95
Umma Party 65, 80, 91, 94
Unionist 91, 216
Unity 33, 81, 112, 160, 203
University of Khartoum 38, 91, 177, 216
Upper Nile 19, 35, 82-3, 97, 110, 136
Ural 167
Ustaz 103
Venn 79
Vice President 11, 17, 39, 54, 100, 110, 156-8, 189-190
Victoria 80
Vilma 53
Vincent 82-83
Wad Medani 46
Wagner 208
Walter 21, 89, 135
Wang 84
Wangari 135
Wanglei 150
Wangulei 18-19
Wani 12, 111, 192
Wantok 33, 38, 111
Wardi 103
Warrap 166
Washington 69, 136-7, 151, 200
Wasila 104
Wat 17, 166
Watergate 137
Wathig 79
Wathiq 14, 103
Watt 83
Wau 27, 30-1, 33, 54, 57, 80, 153, 166
West 99, 109, 146, 169, 200
William 35, 52, 58-9, 80, 88, 102-3, 111, 191, 197
Wol 112
Women 81
Wuor 27
Yaak 52
Yaar 80
Yabus 83
Yach 54-55, 200
Yambio 140-141, 166-7, 171, 173-7
Yasir 16, 104, 106

Yei 70-72, 88, 104, 141, 166
Yemen 199, 202
Yirol 166
Yohannes 34, 47-8, 89
Yong 31, 38, 59, 89
Yor 34, 47-8, 89
Yoruba 131
Yousif 45, 52-3, 62, 102-3, 105-6, 155, 158, 163, 167
Yoweri 22, 124, 130, 135
Yuang 65
Yubo 166, 174-6
Yunis 48-49
Yusuf 43
Zaire 169, 199
Zaki 103
Zambia 135
Zambian 138
Zande 170-171, 177
Zarihun 43
Zenawi 135
Zimbabwe 199
Zink 98, 159

www.ingramcontent.com/pod-product-compliance
Lightning Source LLC
Chambersburg PA
CBHW030548080526
44585CB00012B/303